O'Neil Ford Monograph 3: Fassianos Building

Athens 1990–1995

Kyriakos Krokos

The O'Neil Ford Monograph Series, Volume 3
– Fassianos Building
THE UNIVERSITY OF TEXAS AT AUSTIN
Center for American Architecture and Design
O'Neil Ford Chair in Architecture

Editors
Elias Constantopoulos
Wilfried Wang

Essays
Leti Arvaniti-Krokou
Elias Constantopoulos
Alekos Fassianos
Wilfried Wang

Translation
Elias Constantopoulos

Series Editors
Kevin Alter
Michael Benedikt
Barbara Hoidn
Wilfried Wang

Associate Editors
Daniel Sylvester
Barbara Terrell

Production Editors
Susan McNally
Christine Wong

Design
Daniel Sylvester

Printed and bound in Canada.

Sole Distributor in Europe:
Ernst Wasmuth Verlag GmbH & Co.
Fürststrasse 133
72072 Tübingen, Germany
www.wasmuth-verlag.de
info@wasmuth-verlag.de

ISBN 978-3-8030-0718-6

Sole Distributor in the United States of America and Canada:
D.A.P. / Distributed Art Publishers
155 Sixth Avenue, 2nd Floor
New York, New York 10013, U.S.A.
Tel. (212) 627-1999, Fax. (212) 627-9484

Contents

Acknowledgements

The editors would like to thank the wife of the late Kyriakos Krokos, the architect Leti Arvaniti-Krokou, for generously allowing us to reproduce the drawings and photographs in her archive, as well as for her constant support and contribution to this O'Neil Ford monograph.

Our thanks are equally extended to Alekos Fassianos, the distinguished painter, long time friend, and client of Kyriakos Krokos, who readily opened the doors of the museum and offered valuable insights to its creation. Furthermore, thanks also go to Alekos' brother, the musician Pavlos Fassianos, who furnished us with much additional information regarding construction and history of the building.

We are grateful to Daniel Sylvester, who was responsible for the typography of the book and who showed a deep understanding of the project and a commitment throughout that made the task not only possible but also enjoyable.

Finally, it is particularly gratifying that after 35 years of friendship between the editors, another mutual project, one that celebrates the best of architecture's potential, has come to fruition.

Elias Constantopoulos, Wilfried Wang

Foreword

Fassianos Building

Elias Constantopoulos, Wilfried Wang

For most readers interested in architecture, Kyriakos Krokos (1941–98), if at all known beyond Greece, has been associated with the magnificent Museum of Byzantine Culture (1977, 1989–93) in Thessaloniki. Here, his mastery of materials and detailing was realized in an evocative architecture empathetic of the displayed objects. It would have been more obvious to have dedicated a monograph to this largest building of Krokos had it not been for the fact that the "smaller" projects for the painter Alekos Fassianos (born 1935), Greece' foremost painter, had developed in parallel, if not even anticipated the thinking and designing of the much larger structure. In an age drunken with the belief in ever larger scales, ever taller buildings, and ever grander new cities, this belief in limitless exaggeration has obliterated the foundations of architecture, namely its slow, meticulous, caring, and beautifying craft of making.

It is for this reason that the third O'Neil Ford Monograph turns to Krokos' alteration and renovation of a 1980s apartment building into a private art gallery and apartments. Located at the center of Athens, this was the second intensive commission which Krokos completed for Alekos Fassianos and his extended family following an earlier alteration of a suburban apartment block (1977, 1978–9) that includes Fassianos' atelier. The Fassianos Building at the heart of Athens is being presented as a paradigmatic case for contemporary architectural practice: showing both a respect and understanding for existing built substance and significantly improving it in architectural terms so as to sustain its usefulness for future generations.

Kyriakos Krokos received recognition for his work during his lifetime, but it has only been fully appreciated following his early death. Unquestioningly, Krokos was the outstanding architect of his generation and arguably heir to Dimitris Pikionis, whose love of folk tradition he shared. These traditions not so much encompass their shapes, ornament and colors, but the processes leading up to their coming into being and, most importantly, their life beyond. Krokos was fascinated by the effects of time and climate on buildings. His detailing concerned itself with how things might look well into the future: "Construction is architecture. The thing mustn't spoil or age badly or get dirty; it has to be clean. That would be the ideal. Isn't a pebble ideal? It dries and shines … Or an ancient temple, the part that is washed and is beautiful after the rain has gone? If you don't attend to certain details, how will your work be when it ages and is fragmented … a heap of rubble? Older stone buildings could be rebuilt, something that you can't imagine doing with concrete. You don't discard them; you don't discard the parts of ancient buildings. There's an idea: to make well-fashioned concrete constructions in excavations of ancient ruins. I like the idea of that relationship very much."[1]

Alekos Fassianos and Kyriakos Krokos were close friends. Their kindred spirits are evident in their work: sketched, drawn, painted and built. The mute melancholy brought about by the dashed hopes, simple failures and outright disasters of modern times is evident in Fassianos and Krokos' sketches and paintings. Where a life-affirming, Bacchanalian naïvety appears to be predominant in Fassianos' more widely published work, that impression recedes as the dialogue with Krokos emerges. In Krokos' drawings we see the vast silence of Giorgio de Chirico, the plastic space of Giorgio Morandi and the knowingly futile attempt to retrieve for the benefit of a broader public the spiritual and intellectual basis that gave rise to the great works of Greek Antiquity.
The options for Krokos appeared clear: if the

1. Kyriakos Krokos, interview with Andreas Giacumacatos, *Design + Art in Greece*, no. 27, Athens 1996, p. 23. English transl. *The Architect Kyriakos Krokos*, VI International Exhibition of Architecture: Greece, ed. Andreas Giacumacatos, Venice 1996, p. 25–6.

original aims of enlightenment aesthetics included the return to essentials, then for Krokos, this desire for a *rappel à l'ordre* implied a return to the empathetic power of abstraction as seen amongst others in the sculptures of the Cycladic civlization. Modernists' pretense of an a-historic, "cleansed," ornament-free aesthetic was only credible due to the ignorance of earlier civilizations and the belief in the superiority of Western culture in relation to so-called primitive societies. All that sense of modernist certainty had been shaken by the writings of the Frankfurt School and structural anthropology.

Progress, for Krokos it seems, had to be redefined as being based in the cultivation of base *techné*. This in contrast to Takis Zenetos' (1926–77) research in contemporary technology and its architectural celebration. The tectonic logic of past ages with their frame and infill still held for Krokos. Rather than wood or stone, for Krokos the preferred "contemporary" material and system consisted of reinforced concrete posts and beams, though not in the abstracted, monochromatic manner as pursued by Aris Konstantinidis (1913–93). The surfaces of posts and frames, sometimes of concrete wall panels in Krokos' buildings would be variously tooled to enhance their plasticity, their ability to weather and therefore to accept patina. Moreover, coming from stonemasonry, in which the preparatory process includes the construction of a nominal frame with a marginal line, the socalled draft, we find in all of Krokos' work, whether furniture or architecture, whether tectonic or constructional detail, the notion of the frame (even if occasionally incomplete) with an enclosed field that has been subject to some surface treatment. Thus, what appears almost casually in Krokos' sketches of small houses—the idea of the post and beam—can be retraced in Krokos' architecture: the precise frame of the building, the door, the floor, the opening in the ceiling, the ledge, the threshold, etc.

Engaging reinforced concrete allowed Krokos to reach a hitherto unkown dimension of the precise frame's effect: now the entire continuous structural system could be appropriated in the service of expressing a once ancient and now transcendent conception of architectural order. Using stonemasons' techniques of broaching, pointing, tooth-chiseling, tooling and droving to achieve a dressed finish also on reinforced concrete elements allows for these reinforced concrete elements to be perceived as being closer to stonemasonry than mundane concrete work that more often than not is enveloped in significantly more expensive cladding material. Krokos' architecture is what you see.

The precise frame, the draft, that surrounds a block of stone before it is further dressed, is thus the constructional parallel to the tectonic concept. Importantly, and again in contrast to say Ludwig Mies van der Rohe's (1886–1969) philhellenic sense of the precise frame, Krokos' understanding of the precise frame is dynamic, non-symmetric, picturesque in the same sense as the Erechtheion. It is this balance of the constructional and tectonic notion of the precise frame against the picturesque plasticity that constitutes Krokos' architecture.

By concentrating on the smaller of Krokos' last works, we hope to offer the reader a more comprehensive insight into his approach.

Kyriakos Krokos

Alekos Fassianos

Through his work, Kyriakos Krokos endowed architecture with a national conscience. This he achieved without imitating the past that had been his teacher.

He looked at and studied vernacular architecture: the small Mediterranean island houses, which, bathed in light, connect a person to antiquity. His architecture calms you and guides you through the atriums and the small terraces it creates, towards these same memories of light. He wanted the houses that he built to be in no need of upkeep with the passage of time. He used to tell me that a building must be like a pebble on the beach, which gets covered with sand before the wave comes and washes it off.

Krokos (left) and Fassianos on the building site
Athens, 1995

He used to worry when he saw badly formed concrete on building sites. They would say to him, "It does not matter, it will be plastered over afterwards." He would answer that it would resemble an old woman with lots of make-up on her face. He wanted the structure of the building to be evident, that it be understandable in the way in which it was constructed. He said that when an ancient building is demolished, beautiful pieces are always left behind, whereas in contemporary buildings nothing of value is left. The drums of an ancient column remain. That is the architecture he wished for: everything to be visible in daylight.

Kyriakos Krokos, *Imaginary Landscape*,
crayons and gouache

Essay

Fassianos Building

Wilfried Wang

Architects' conventional understanding of their task is to build something new, ideally on a free, unencumbered site. In this way, an architectural design is revealed in all its three-dimensional glory. The concept behind the building emerges unperturbed. Its formal elaboration can be photographically captured while the architect can present the building in its entirety without requiring any editorial effort at excluding unwanted objects.

It is preeminent extrovert architects who believe in such an uncompromised representation of their ideas. They have a clear penchant for such commissions. In this way, they feel their egos embodied in the building. For extrovert architects, the opposite of maximum outward self-manifestation is the renovation of an existing building. Extrovert architects find these types of commissions altogether constraining, not to say boring. In these commissions, the context needs to be respected. Even worse for extrovert architects is a protective framework, such as a group of buildings or a single building in which all the details and the overall form has been placed under conservation for reasons of historical or architectural value. Most architects, including extrovert architects, feel that these conditions severely restrict their freedom of expression.

However, if truth be told, no absolutely free, a-contextual commissions exist. There are always defining circumstances including, most obviously these: the site, the topography, the prevailing climate, the solar aspect, the soil condition, and flora or fauna that have made the location their habitat. There are planning and building codes, liens and covenants, infrastructural restrictions, paths, roads and air rights. There are the non-physical discourses within the profession, some more deeply grounded, others more fashionable. There are local, regional, national, and international cultures to consider. And then there are all the skulking thoughts in the architects' heads, bursting to be freed, having had to wait years before being set loose. Few restrictions have a greater effect on creativity than human imagination itself. Imagination constitutes the true design context for architects. It is only this recognition of the conceptual limits of architectural exploration that sets the creative mind free.

Thus the complaint—raised against the notion of context as that anachronistic and stifling corset to creativity—is often directed at the "others," the restrictive external forces. However, the notion of context is broader and simultaneously more restrictive. The notion of context is not merely confined to the external or the concrete, but to the conceptual and psychological. Between these extremes, between the external physical realm and the internal psychological one is where a truly creative act can occur; here an intention condenses into an ideal typical paradigm, turning an architectural design into an instance of an integral reality, a piece of the world on its own terms.

Rather than fighting phantoms of the constraining context kind, Kyriakos Krokos (1941–98) adapted an existing 1980s seven story mixed-use building in Athens into an art gallery and apartments in such a way that the building's previous banal character was utterly transformed into one of restrained grace. Krokos' redesign uncovered latent qualities of the 1980s building while also remodeling it—an approach that is comparable to a sculptor's ability of seeing inside a raw block of stone a potential figure, beguilingly lifelike. So, this is the case for any architectural task: to understand the inner and outer constraints as a raw block of stone from which Galatea is wrought. The designer's perspicacity is required to penetrate all of these constraints in order to imagine an animated essence. In the best sense, architectural design brings inert matter to life.

To which kind of life is this inert matter brought? If it is true that architecture is the one form of art that intervenes in and constitutes reality, then the character of this life that architecture seeks is conscious, particular and dedicated. Krokos made a clear choice when he transformed the 1980s apartment building. The resultant architectural design respects the majority of the existing fabric of the pre-existing multi-story dwelling, while changing only very small wall and floor sections and creating a few new openings and closing others, thereby tuning the compositional syntax: revealing the hitherto buried stonework of the party wall; screening the bulk of the upper facade by the new balcony grid; integrating new kitchens and bathrooms; and otherwise ennobling the building with wooden door frames, marble ledges and windows sills, bronze balustrade panels, and other considered details.

In this sense, the different degrees of rusticity of the brick, stone and concrete walls, each with their specific texture and color, meet the variety of honed and polished floor surfaces, which, when seen together, create a harmonious mellifluousness. Krokos made use of the changing degree of roughness and refinement of the party wall from the lower to the upper level as a self-explanatory index of loads. At a detailed level, Krokos employed archaic, stepped sections in the walls of the lower gallery level to accentuate the stacking effect.

The basic idea of the load support is also visible on the exterior. While the original engineer-designed apartment block had a single continuous balcony above the mezzanine level and a number of shorter, normal length balconies on the two street facades (thereby allowing the street wall to read as the dominant plane), the new reinforced concrete balcony grid designed by Krokos created a veil to this upper section of the building. What had appeared rather dumb now has a more filigree character. With this, Krokos achieved two things at the same time: the now unified apartments are understood to be located distinctly on top of the mute, seemingly monolithic gallery base, yet, thanks to the balcony, the building volume containing the apartments appears light.

The urban obliviousness of the 1980s version of the functional apartment building with its minimal window frames, matter-of-fact proportions and indistinct surfaces was subjugated to a synthetic reformation reminiscent of Dimitris Pikionis' late works for the landscape around

the Acropolis and the Philopappos Hill (1951–57, 1954–57), a design that is marked by a synthesis of calligraphic concrete elements merging with polygonal stonework and the odd abstracted classical architectural motif. The renovated Fassianos Building equally holds in high regard the power of anonymous vernacular forms—their indebtedness to classical origins and their realization in coarse but true materials. Integrated within these expansive wall and floor surfaces are Fassianos' reliefs, engravings, and murals; occasionally miniature sculptures, such as a small bust at the bottom of the handrail in the gallery or the relief-like sculpture of a man on a pedestal on the mezzanine gallery, are unassumingly displayed.

These integrated works of art provide the connection to the temporary display in the Fassianos' private gallery. The larger part of Fassianos' work consists of work on paper or paintings. These are shown in a traditional way, hanging on walls. A metal rod hanging system enables exhibitions to be changed with ease.

Given the restrictive dimensions of the plot, the former retail space, now turned into the introverted central exhibition space, has two contiguous walls that create a sense of enclosure. At the lower ground floor, the sense of enclosure is slightly greater, thanks to the third contiguous wall (containing the archive). There are no classical rooms or museum-like spaces; Krokos kept the gallery spaces altogether quite open. In part, this sense of openness is achieved by means of the two triple height spaces at both ends of the building: one containing the steel staircase with frosted glazing at ground level, the other below the courtyard skylight.

Both triple height spaces are sources of richly nuanced indirect light. This contrasts with the artificial lighting system which provides light from a clerestory slot. This system is less successful as it is the cause of more glare than indirect light reflection off the ceiling.

The courtyard skylight is an enlargement of the previous one at the same location. However, in its redesigned trapezoidal geometry it helps to diminish the spatial effect of the non-parallel outer walls, an effect that is achieved as a result of the perspectival regularization of the non-orthogonal space. Similarly, the triple height opening of the staircase aids in the perception of the overall space being based on a rectangle: it too is actually set in a trapezoidal plan.

Within the apartment units, Krokos deals with this issue in different ways, sometimes using poché walls, sometimes using quarter curves in the walls to suggest a more straightforward geometry. For it is not until the plans are seen that the building's actual non-orthogonal shape is understood. While the original building already conforms to some basic planning restrictions (maximum building height and minimum setback), the location of the vertical core has been efficiently placed to provide maximum freedom in the use of the remaining space.

The apartments themselves have distinct characters. Above the mezzanine gallery lays Fassianos' own "apartment," connected to the exhibition space via a ladder-like stair. Of the four units, the character of Fassianos' apartment is the most formal. This formality is established by means of the almost axially symmetric positioning of the openings, in detail emphasized by their frames of finely pointed

The old covered atrium (above, left) and the new atrium with skylight (above, right), Fassianos' Building, Kyriakos Krokos, 1990–95

gray reinforced concrete or mahogany-stained door and window sets. From this apartment, access is gained to the large roof terrace, surrounded on two sides with a masonry bench. The terrazzo floor of the apartment interior, framed by white marble from Nestos, is extended to the terrace, here in a finely tooled finish, thereby creating a matte, non-slip surface. Towards the exterior, a small, rounded balcony with a split balustrade, marked by a pair of doves in relief, overlooks the street. The generosity of the apartment and terrace is established by the large opening with the sliding full-height glass doors that can be made to disappear into wall pockets. At this level, private receptions can take place and works of art can be shown in an art gallery-like manner (otherwise kept in the tall storage cupboards on the exterior wall).

The four upper units were originally conceived to accommodate different members of the family. Though the floor plate is relatively small, the variety and nuances in layout are noteworthy. In essence, the large room at the center and the kitchen/bathroom in the shorter wing to the west are constants. The intermediate units are characteristic of more formal sensibilities with individual rooms being given a sense of symmetric poise. Only the attic unit with its minimal interior and maximal roof terrace is reminiscent—in compositional terms and a few details—of modernist precedents (Eileen Gray and Jean Badovici at E.1027, Roquebrune sur mer, for example).

In a way, the tectonic order of heavy to light from the lower to upper levels—as seen in the treatment of masonry and reinforced concrete—is paralleled in the changes in character of the architecture from the more archaic at the lower level to the modern at the attic, albeit screened on the exterior by the two balcony grids.

Thus, from a distance, it can be seen that Krokos eradicated the 1980s banality of the engineer-designed apartment building in as much as a sculptor is compelled to demolish the outer surface of a block of stone to reach the perceived inherent figure. Seen close-up, the few small changes in substance and the significant changes in the character of the building (principally achieved through careful syntactic corrections and elaborate honing of surfaces) have given the former building an entirely new life. To paraphrase Adolf Loos' definition of an architect as a mason who has learned to speak Latin, Krokos has given the former engineer-designed apartment building a course in stonemasonry.

Indeed, it is Krokos' knowledge of and fascination with stonemasonry—its ability to strike life into surfaces of stones and of concrete—that constitutes this "learning" process for the 1980s building. Krokos transposed the principles of stonemasonry to the preparation and surface treatment of the tectonic components, the posts and beams, the walls and floors. Given that traditional stonemasonry deals with blocks of stone that are, at the most, no larger than a person, Krokos' use of reinforced concrete allows the appropriation of the stonemason's craft to the scale of a tectonic element. For example, he utilized this method by casting the entire height of a post, thereby monumentalizing that tectonic element—something that had not seemed conceivable since the end of neo-classicism.

However, such monumentalization occurs only in a few instances: the monolithic exterior base of the building, thereby marking the gallery volume; at a smaller scale, the single column at the front entrance with its capital merging with the similarly finished beam; and the door frames, both on the outside and in some of the apartments. The stipple effect on the surface of the reinforced concrete is achieved with masonry tools; it is a somewhat finer finish than bush-hammering but coarser than tooled or drove work.

The syntactic discipline imposed by a course in Latin could be said to have its equivalent in the process of working stone. From the extraction of coarse blocks of stone from a quarry to the gradual preparation of individual pieces for a building there are numerous working stages. Having reached the final overall dimensions, regardless of the finish of the facing surface, traditionally the stonemason chisels a framing margin or draft around the face. This frame is often left visible in the finished work. It is this frame that is visible at different scales on the

edges of constructional and tectonic elements in Krokos' architecture.

Over the years, Krokos had been working with transposed stonemason's techniques. Thus a conceptual concatenation appears to have taken place in Krokos' understanding of frame and surface, being extended across reinforced concrete elements altogether. The underlying discipline of design is marked by the consistent framing of the surface to be dressed: the draft in stonemasonry, the marble edging framing the terrazzo floor, the stippled reinforced concrete frame to the passageway, the reinforced concrete grid to the balconies. Krokos applies the principle of the precise frame, sometimes in a symmetric, on other occasions in an asymmetric, picturesque way, thereby extending the stonemason's precision across the constructional scale to the level of a tectonic order. If one would like, one could see the overall treatment of the building's configuration in this light: the smooth corners and edges of the building itself can be read as the "draft" framing the balcony grid as the "dressed" surface, akin to a stone block's surface treatment.

The Fassianos Building is a paradigm in the knowing, corrective intervention within an existing building in formal and spatial syntactic terms, combined with an intensive and precise crafting of surfaces. Krokos' approach synthesizes the grand knowledge of architecture with the continued cultivation of stonemason's *techné*. In this work, detailing and composition are related, interconnected and mutually supportive. This work establishes a credible relation between conception and materialization. It is substantive.

Essay

Kyriakos Krokos and the Fassianos Museum

Leti Arvaniti-Krokou

The intention of the well-known painter Alekos Fassianos to create a museum for his paintings, brought great joy to his friend Kyriakos Krokos, because Krokos knew he would be a candidate for the project. The location had not yet been determined and the possibility of the museum being a new building caused great anticipation for Krokos. At some point Alekos Fassianos expressed his desire to build the museum in the place of his parental family house, near the main Larissis Train Station in Athens, which had been already replaced by a low-cost apartment building. This area was considerably degraded by then, but its relative proximity to the Archaeological Museum and the School of Architecture seemed to be an asset.

Krokos faced a great dilemma, and he was ambivalent for some time before deciding whether he would undertake the reconstruction of this poorly built apartment building, located in a dense and complex part of Athens. He would have to completely transform the building in order to achieve a result that would correspond both to his expectations and to its purpose to be a museum! In order to understand the difficulty and importance of this decision, consider that Krokos devoted himself to everything he agreed to create; he would be entirely dedicated to the project, working on it until he believed that the building was properly completed and he was satisfied with the outcome. The challenge of such a project, in addition to his friend and artist Fassianos being an employer, was of great importance. Thus today we have the building presented in this book.

The discussions for the Fassianos Museum started in 1990, and the construction was completed by 1995. The brief on the spatial requirements was quickly decided upon.

The ground floor, together with the mezzanine and the basement level would serve as the main area of the museum, closed off and protected from noisy Metaxa Street. The dominant elements for linking these three levels are the metal staircase and a skylight and atrium that begins on the mezzanine level and runs vertically through the museum until it reaches the basement, integrating the three levels with natural light. The first floor above the mezzanine, with its internal courtyard and apartment, was where the artist Fassianos was to live and work.

The second, third, and fourth floors above this apartment were apartments for the three brothers of Fassianos (musicians Andreas and Pavlos and the actor Spyros), well accommodated within the overall building design.

A major concern in the project was the design of the elevations so they could signal the unique use of the building. Krokos had the idea of uniting the small pre-existing balconies into one unified whole in order to create a plexus between the apartments. This second surface layer, formed by vertical columns and horizontal beams of hammered concrete, both distinguishes the museum levels from the upper apartments while also differentiating the building from the surrounding ones; it is now mainly characterized by its new vertical disposition.

At the start of the project Krokos made only the necessary drawings for planning permission, including the plans of the existing building, were made in collaboration with Krokos' associates, the architect Yota Kalavritinou, and the civil engineer Yannis Tsopanakis. The project was

simply entitled "Intervention to the apartment building elevations, without interior alterations." Everything else was realized on site. During construction Melina Chadjiyannouli was the collaborating architect.

The unmasking and the revelation of the load-bearing structure took place first and then followed the addition and the removal of all other elements according to the construction and formal requirements.

Already for Kyriakos Krokos, the building had been preceded by other important projects, such as the theater on Cykladon Street, the apartment building in Aghia Paraskevi, the Vettas residence in Athens, and the Museum of Byzantine Culture in Thessaloniki, which was in the last stage of completion. These tests had been completed, and Krokos was in a more mature phase of architectural creativity; he was closer to what he wanted to pursue and was now ready to further explore unknown territories. Krokos and his excellent crew of workmen/craftsmen composed in tandem this piece of work. A long-term relationship existed between them. They knew him, and he knew them; they learned from him, and he learned from them. They maintained among themselves an excellent resonance. Only a few craftsmen worked on this building along with a couple of able workmen. They are worth mentioning at this point:

Panagiotis Tsiakoumis, the builder and one of the most experienced craftsmen who had worked with Krokos for a long time, was able to handle the stones and the bricks with great expertise. He was also in charge of forming and shaping the exposed concrete, into its multiplicity of textures and finishes.

Giorgos Panou was responsible for the construction of the balcony plexus out of reinforced concrete. Leonidas Diveris knew

many different techniques of hammering and tooling concrete and taught other able workmen in their application.

Dionissis Petas, the carpenter, was always faithfully following instructions, never transgressing them. He brought the window frames painted only with primer, and when Krokos and Fassianos saw them they liked them as they were, deciding that this should be their final color. Within the context of the true nature of materials and the avoidance of coatings, they eschewed using paint which they believed created a superficial skin that could peel off easily.

Fotis Vatelis, the stone mason, laid, almost on his own, all the marble floor slabs in the building. One day Krokos went with him to the Archaeological Museum so that they could see the way the marble skirting was used and how it was applied in the various halls in order to comprehend its character in terms of its dimensions. He was also very inventive regarding the curved skirting of the apartment building staircase. In addition, he successfully undertook the installation of all the mosaic (terrazzo).

Dimitris Chatziorfanos, the blacksmith, manufactured the metal staircase for the museum, which seems to be floating. At the same time, it is inscribed within an irregular space and it was very difficult for Chatziorfanos to find its exact imprint on plan. One day he invited us to his workshop; he was very satisfied with what he had accomplished, so we all went there and admired his work. He manufactured the metal casings, the main entrance door of the museum, and all the rails and banisters, in sheet and woven form. When the bronze sheet panels were placed in the balconies, a brief panic occured—the whole building was glowing, it had turned gold. He assured us that soon the bronze would turn black, as indeed it did.

In the entire building, the natural, earthen materials are quite distinct.

At 7:30 every morning, Krokos would be present at the construction site (the *yapi*) to give out instructions before going to the next site for supervision. Most of the time he stayed there for the whole day until all the workmen had left. He had to observe how things were done, to discuss matters, to ask for our opinion even when he was certain about something to avoid any mistakes, to take care of something he did not think of at first or that he did not like; he was very strict about those matters, he never stepped back. If he didn't like something he would literally pull it down. He experimented...it was orgasmic!

He resolved every issue on site and instructions to the craftsmen regarding the more complex matters that arose were sketched on the walls, in addition to the detailed drawings that were prepared at the office.

Fassianos and Krokos discussing in the *yapi*, colored by Fassianos, undated

A sample was prepared for everything, be it the color of the mortar grout on the stone wall, the color of pressed plaster (applied by specialist crafstman Takis Glykiotis), the composition, size and color of the inlaid marble chips in the mosaic floors, the size and the color of the concrete's aggregates, the many different types of hammering, the height of the marble skirting inside the museum, the doorknobs and much more. When the sampling process was complete, it was still very difficult for Krokos to make a decision; he was frustrated; he believed that there is a golden section in everything and that if you miss it, even with the slightest deviation, you may disrupt the harmony of the whole and end up with something awkward or ungainly.

The recreation of the apartment building was a long-lasting labor. Almost daily Fassianos would visit, usually along with friends, to take part in this quest. They would stand together. At some point, one of them would say something, then the other would add something else, "what do you think about this," "do you like it," "how should we proceed with this," and so on.
In the final stage, the architect Giorgos Fatseas carried out the study of the building lighting. The fact that the museum would be created within an already existing building, where many elements could not be changed (e.g., the floor height, the location of the main staircase) was, in my opinion, the spark that drove Kyriakos Krokos' architectural intervention. The diversification in the significance of the whole building, as was well as of all its parts and spaces, comes to the fore due to the particularly meticulous design and elaboration of materials, which in the courtyard extends to include the neighboring apartment building walls.

This special treatment of the materials is apparent when one looks from the street in front of the two main entrances: the color of the small pebbles (the aggregates) in the concrete of the entrance to the museum is different from the one used in the entrance to the apartment building; the concrete is also hammered differently. The column between them is smooth, so that if it is touched by a passer-by, the feel will be pleasant.

In the Fassianos building, the element of abstraction is dominant, as is the lack of a decorative mood, even if at first glance someone might claim the exact opposite. However, there was always a clear reason for doing everything in this way and not in a different one or why something was placed at an exact location and not a little bit further, and so on. All it takes for someone to realize this is to observe closely with interest.

Whenever we were in the countryside, on Aegina Island, or on Samos Island, Kyriakos would observe the walls of the stockyards, the dry walls, the old stone walls; he would photograph them and comment on the kind of the stone, the different ways of building, the grouts. He would be interested with the wall as a whole. In the well-built ones he would discern the thought behind them, the neatness, the care, the wisdom, and he would accredit them with the appropriate significance.

A similar feeling of fulfillment infuses and follows me every time I walk inside this building, showing me that the thought and the care given in every possible part of the museum, is reflected and embraces me.

The Fassianos Museum is the last building completed by Kyriakos Krokos. My wish is that it will have a life of its own, that it will at some point start to function properly, that people will go in and out of it and share this joy, feel this unique emotion that it evokes to its few visitors today.

Stone wall on Aegina island.

52

Sketches & Drawings

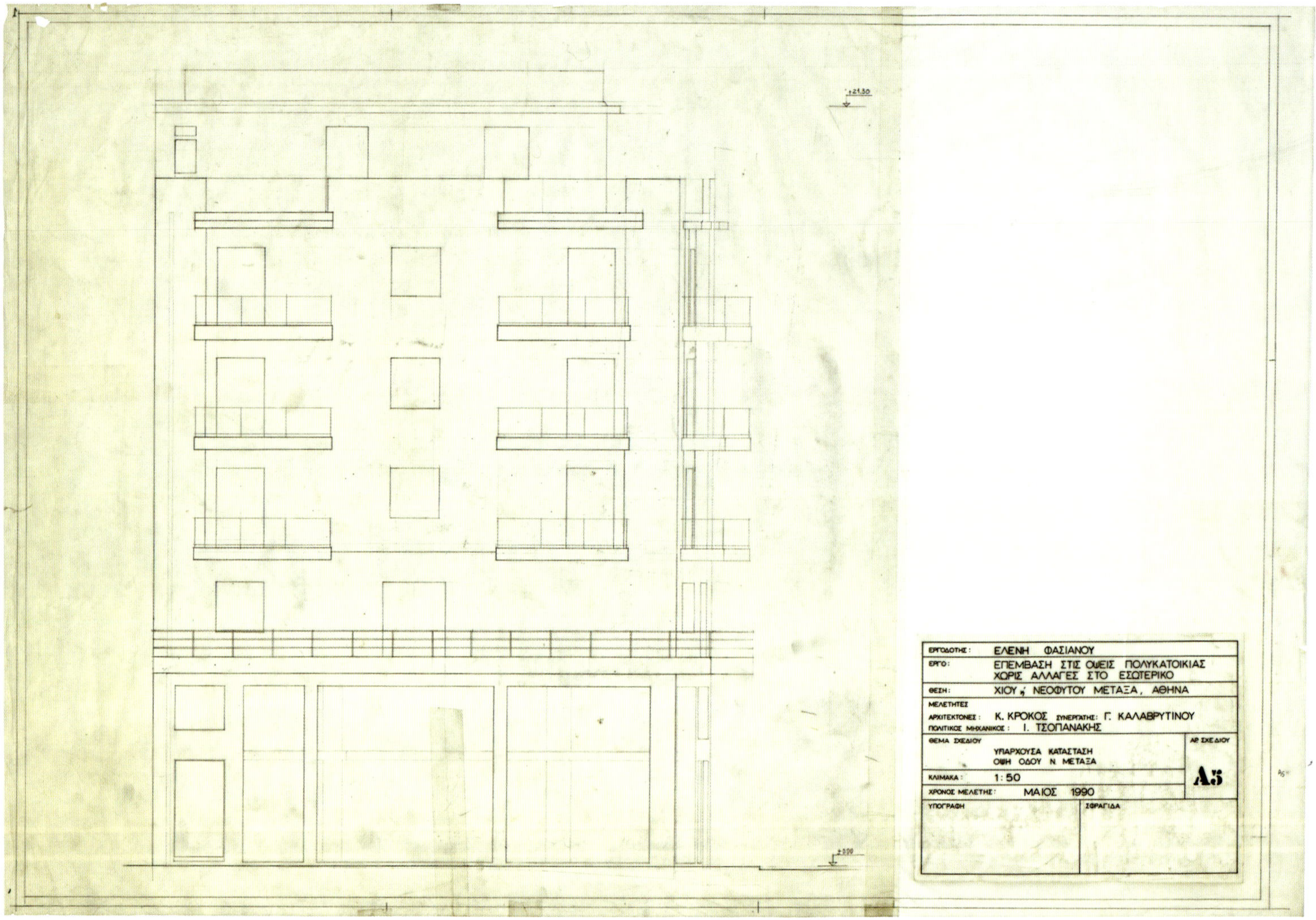

Previous spread: drawing of clerestory windows in main gallery
Above: existing elevation, Metaxa Street, 1990, not to scale
Opposite page: preliminary sketches for Metaxa Street elevation

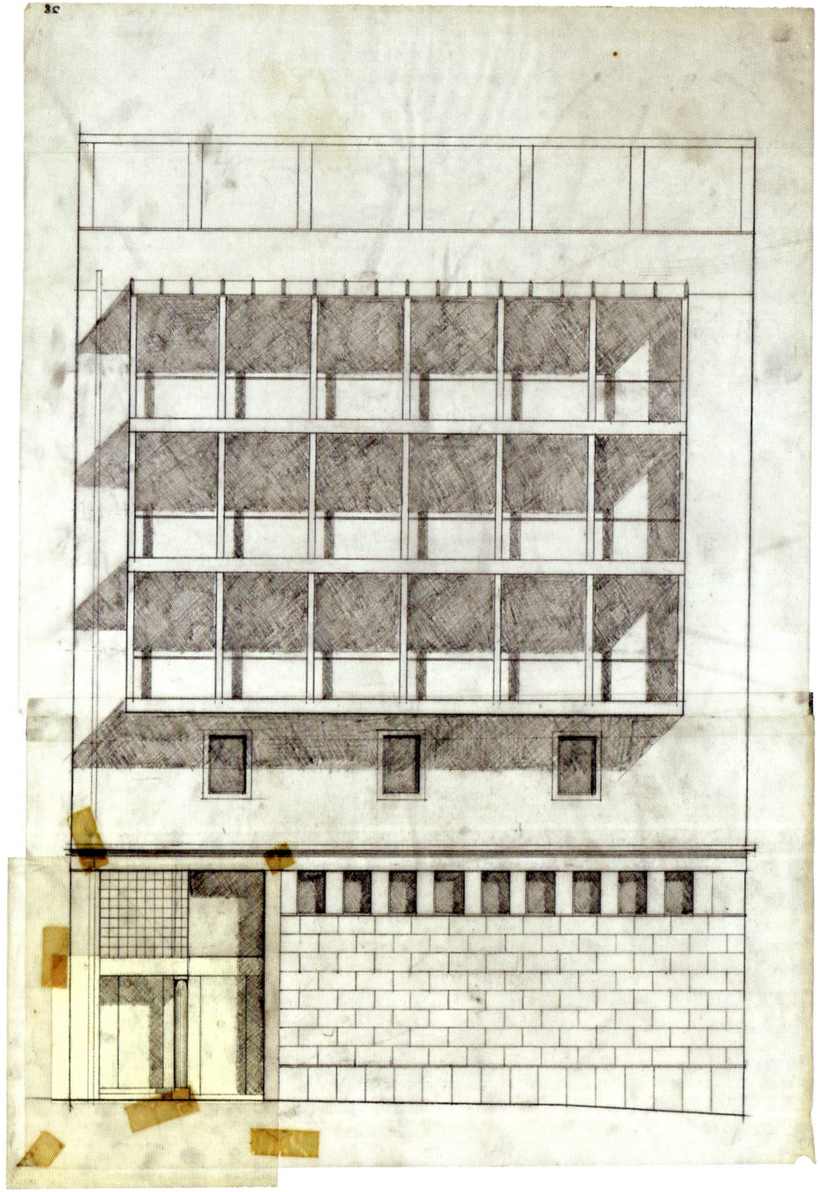

Proposals for new elevation, Metaxa Street

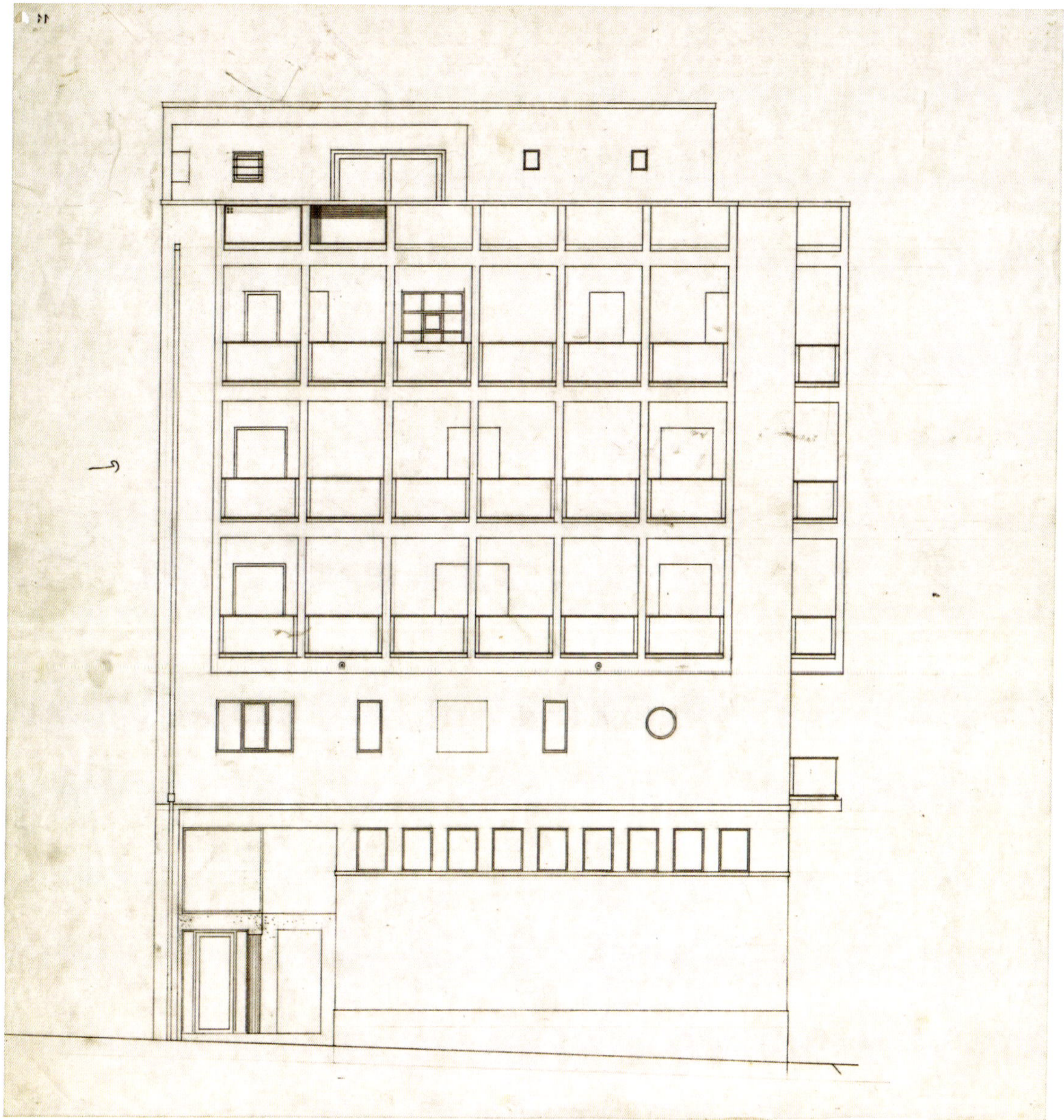

New elevation, Metaxa Street

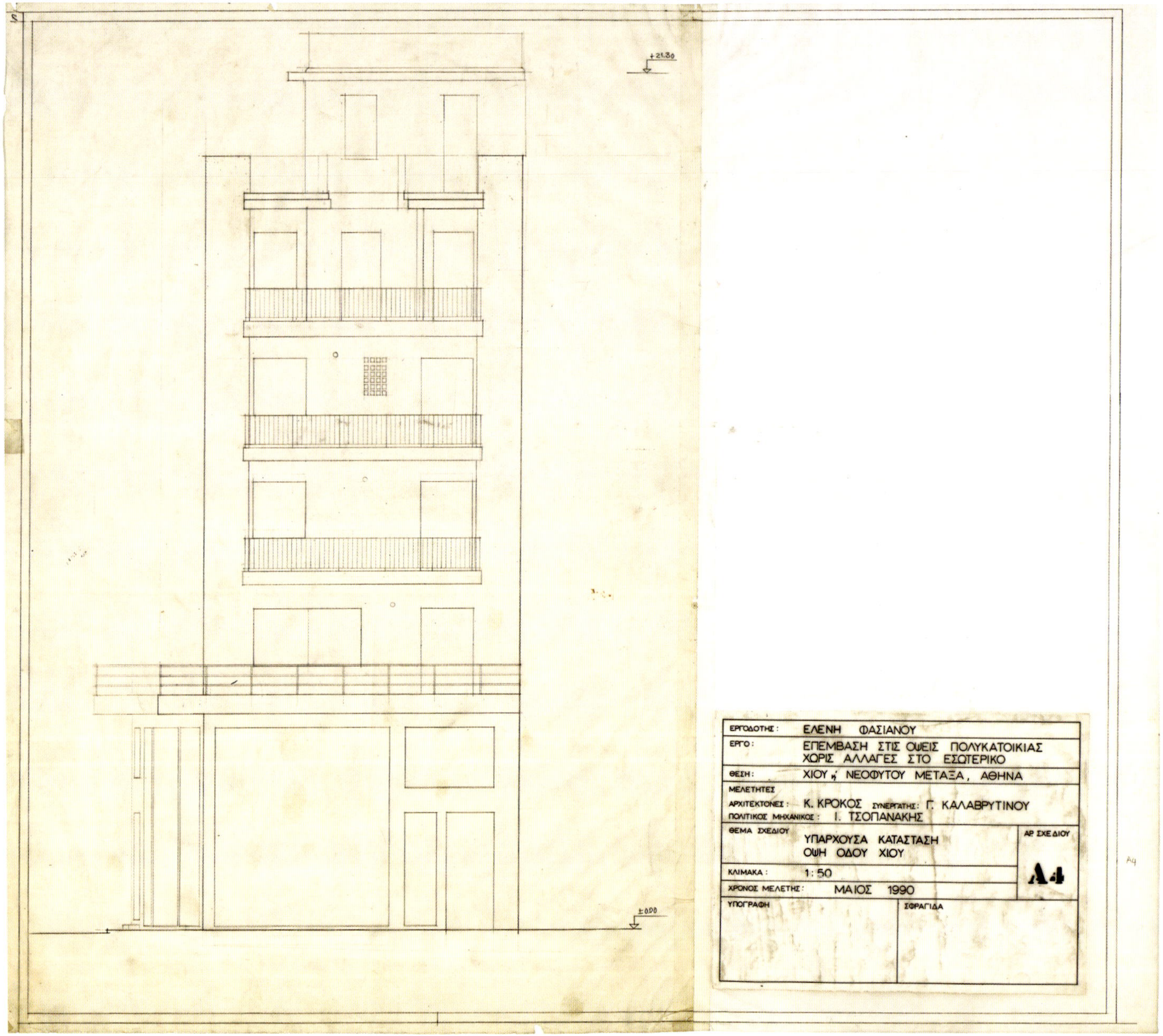

Existing elevation, Chiou street, 1990, not to scale

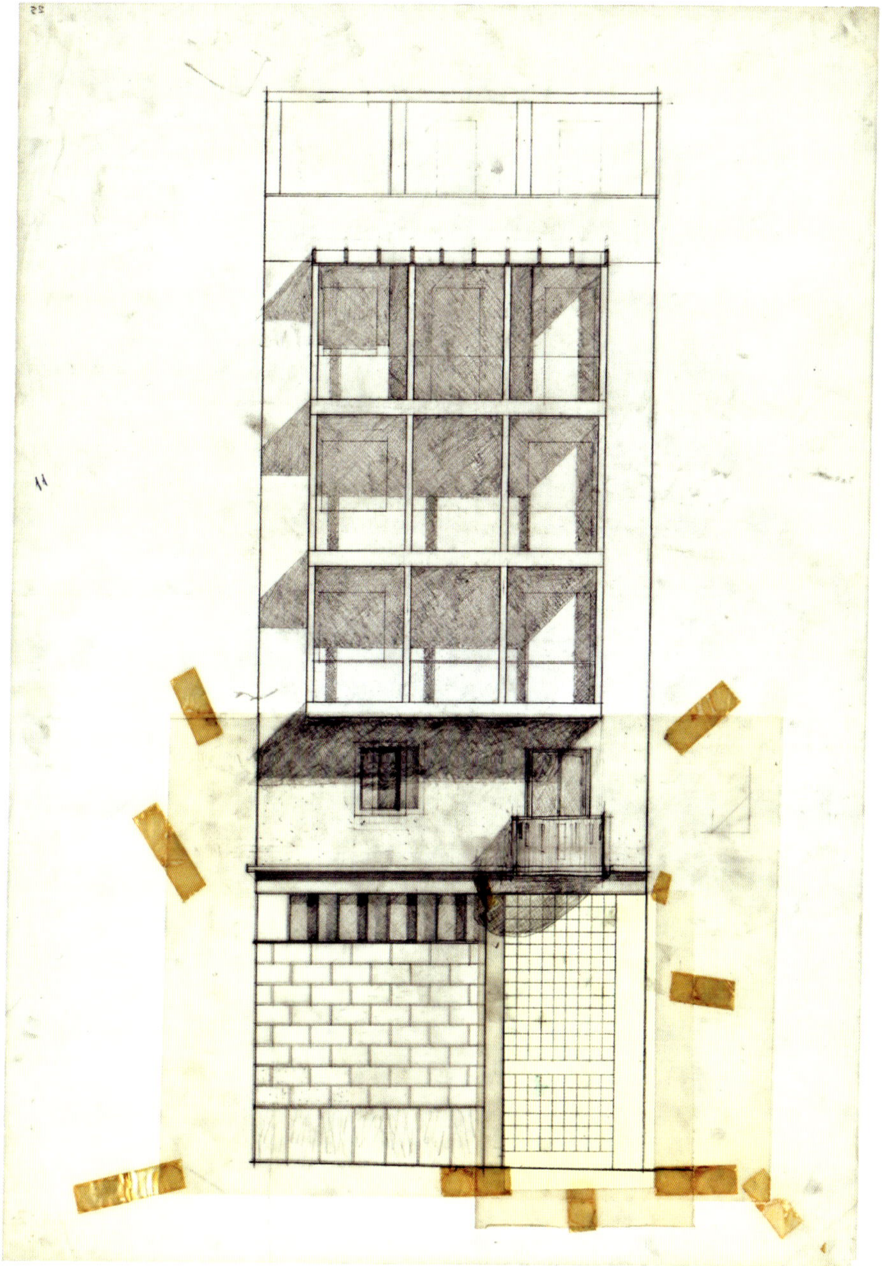

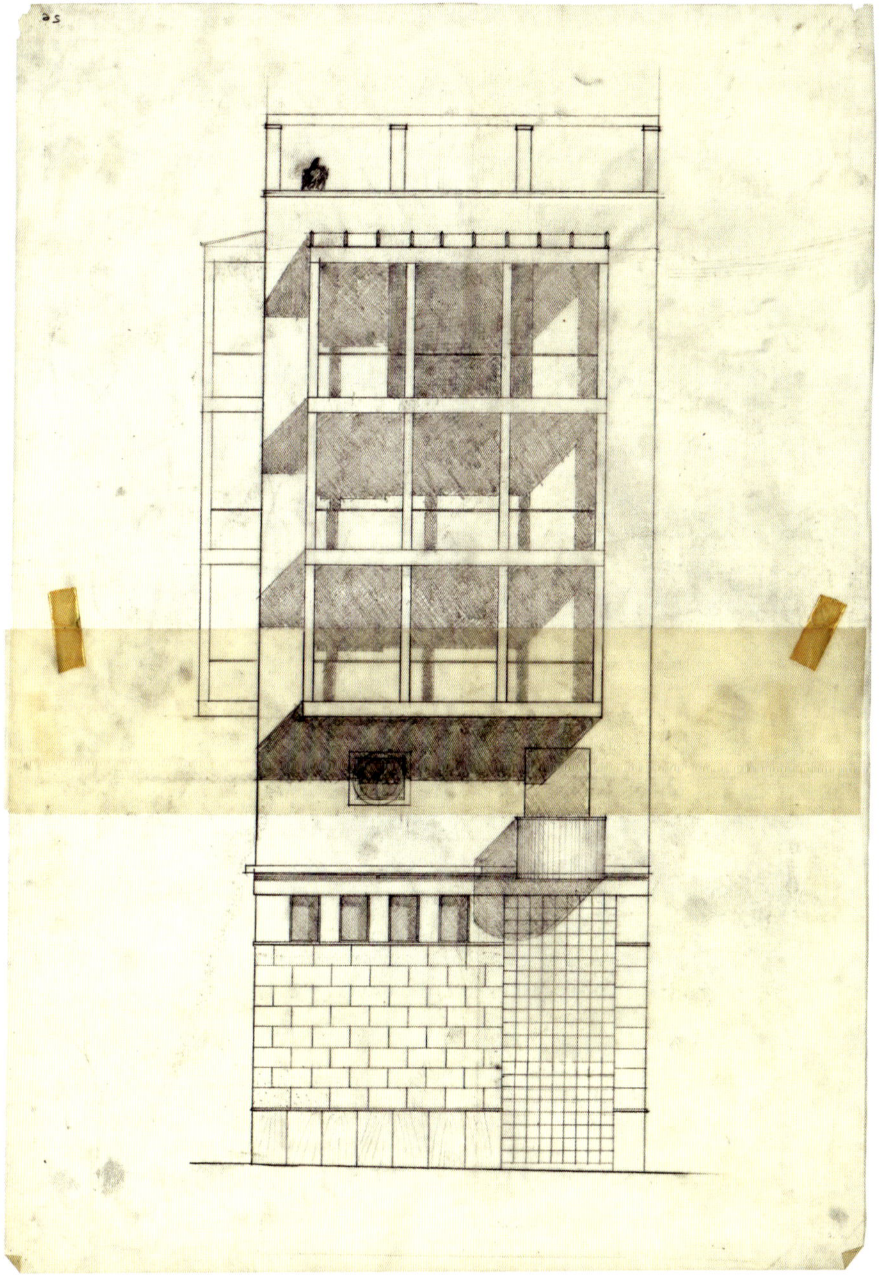

Proposals for new elevation, Chiou street

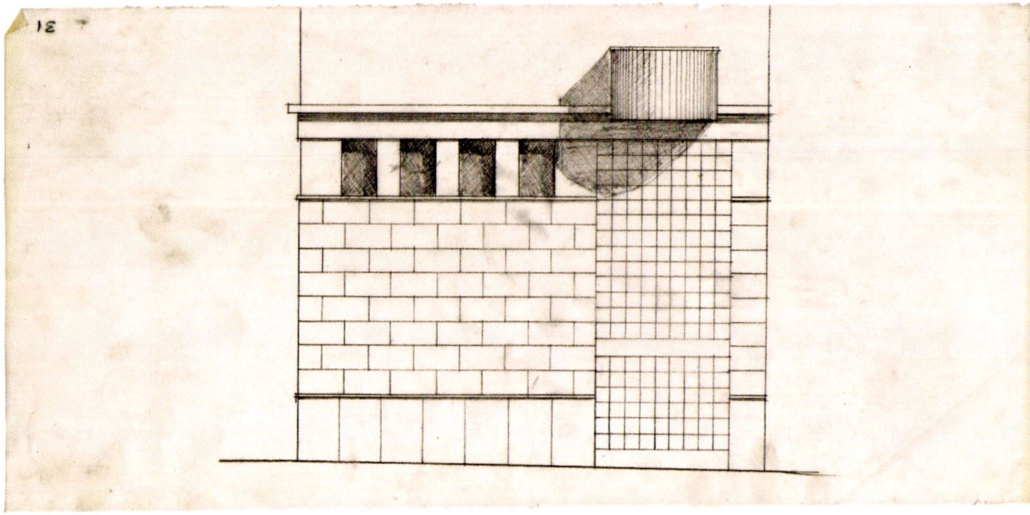

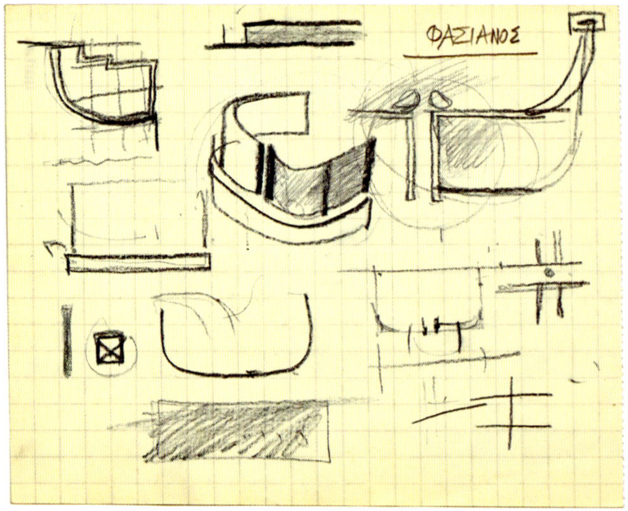

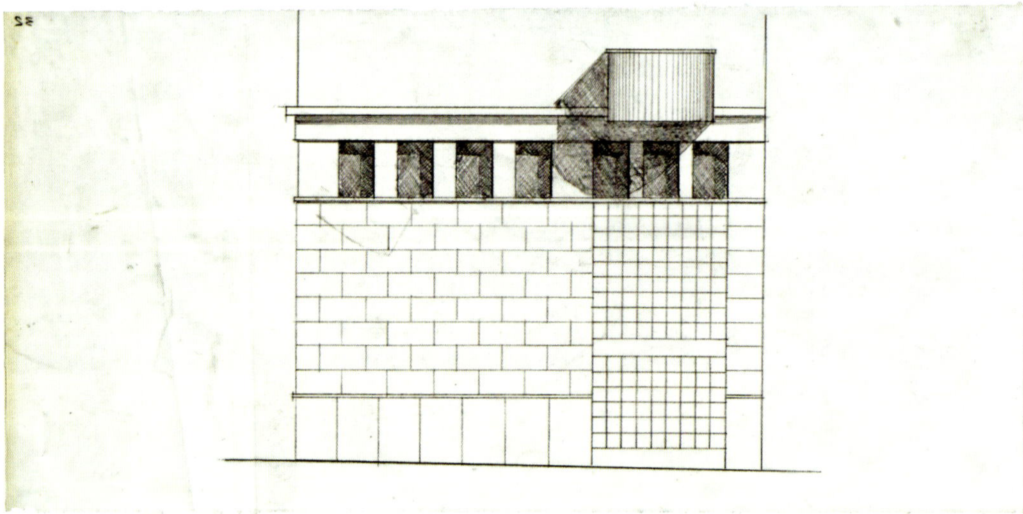

Lower left: sketches of first floor balcony,
Upper and lower right: proposals for ground floor gallery elevation, Chiou Street

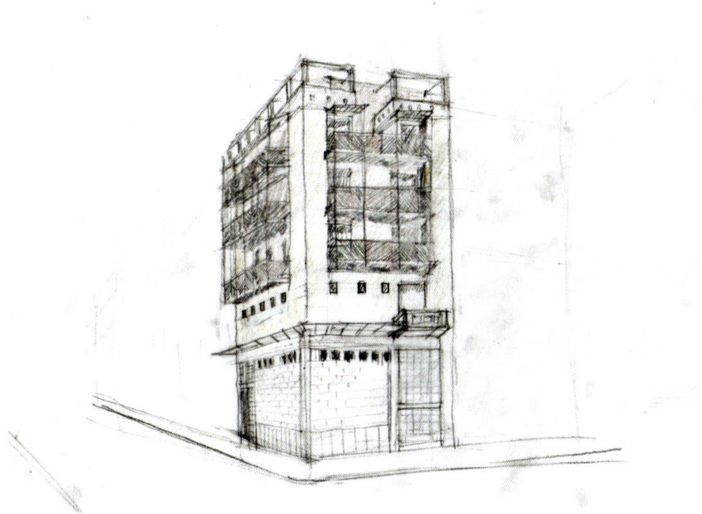

Lower left: apartment building and gallery entrance sketch,
Upper right: preliminary sketch for building

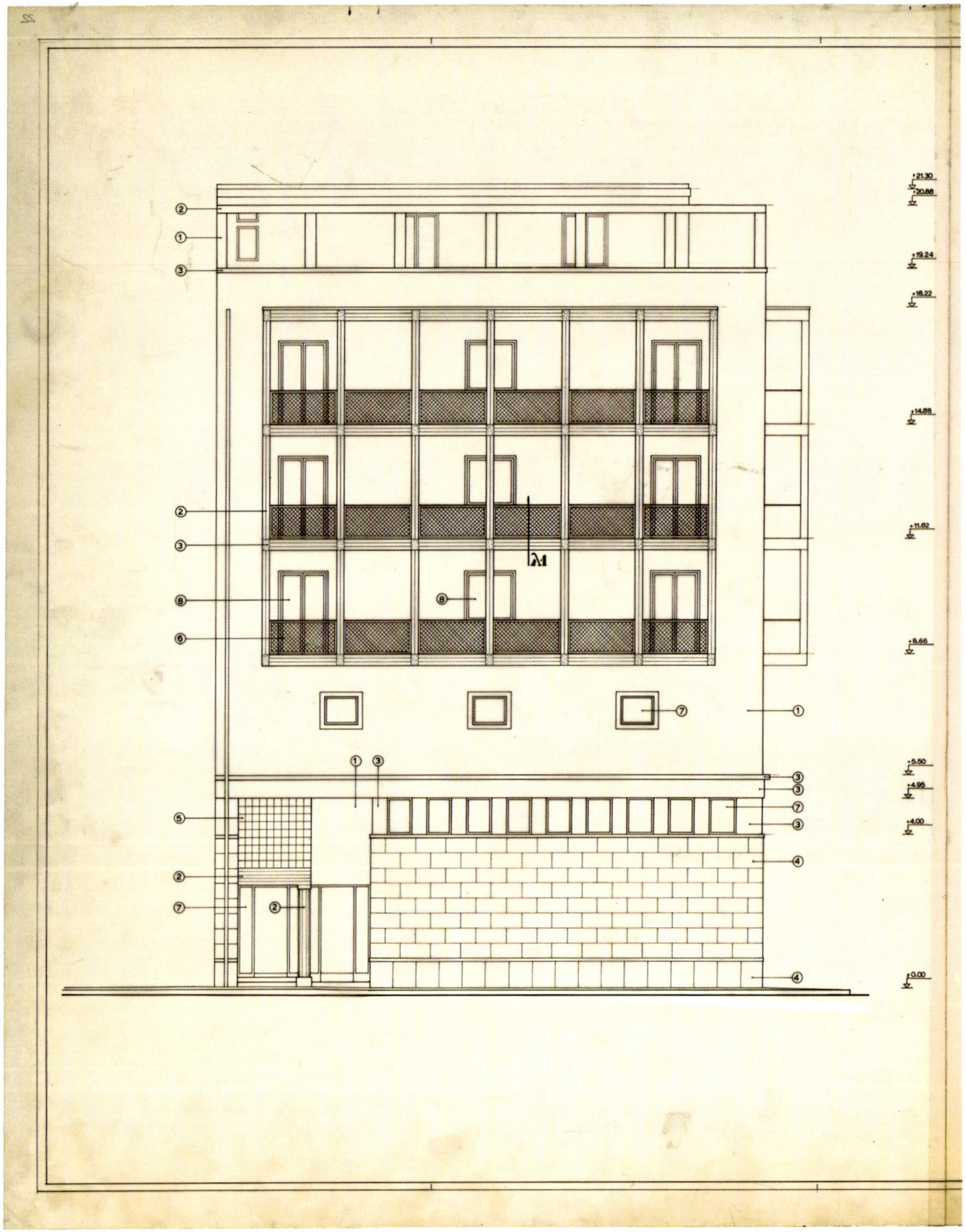

+21.30
+20.88
+19.24
+18.22
+14.88
+11.82
+8.66
+5.50
+4.95
+4.00
±0.00

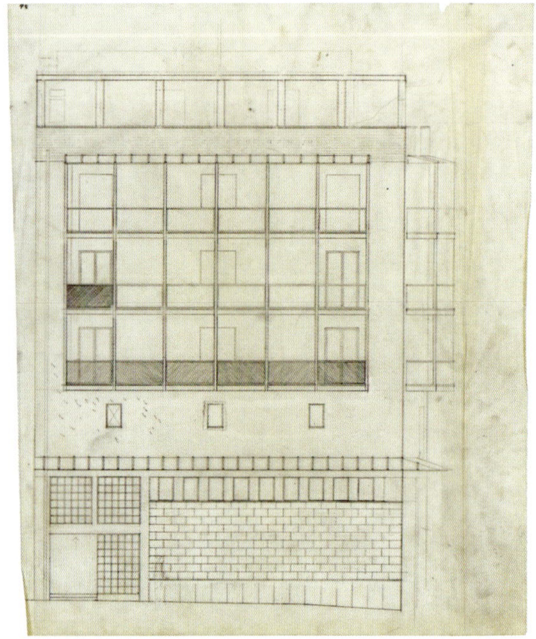

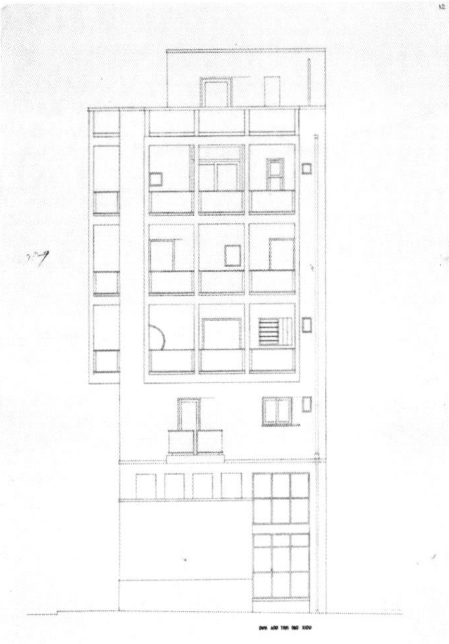

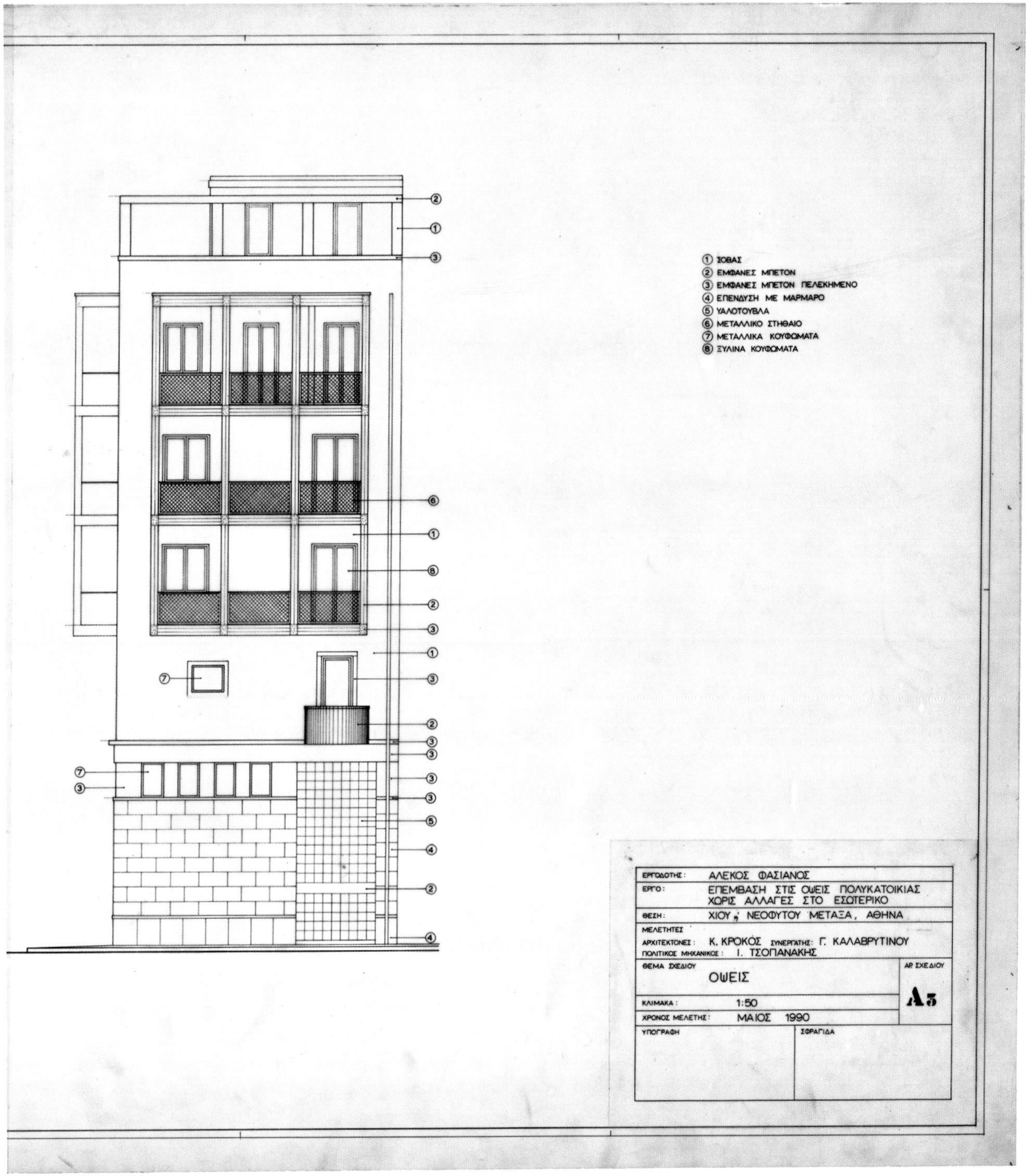

Clockwise from far left, opposite page:
planning permission elevation, Metaxa Street, 1990; proposal for new Metaxa Street elevation; proposal for new Chiou Street elevation; planning permission elevation, Chiou street, 1990

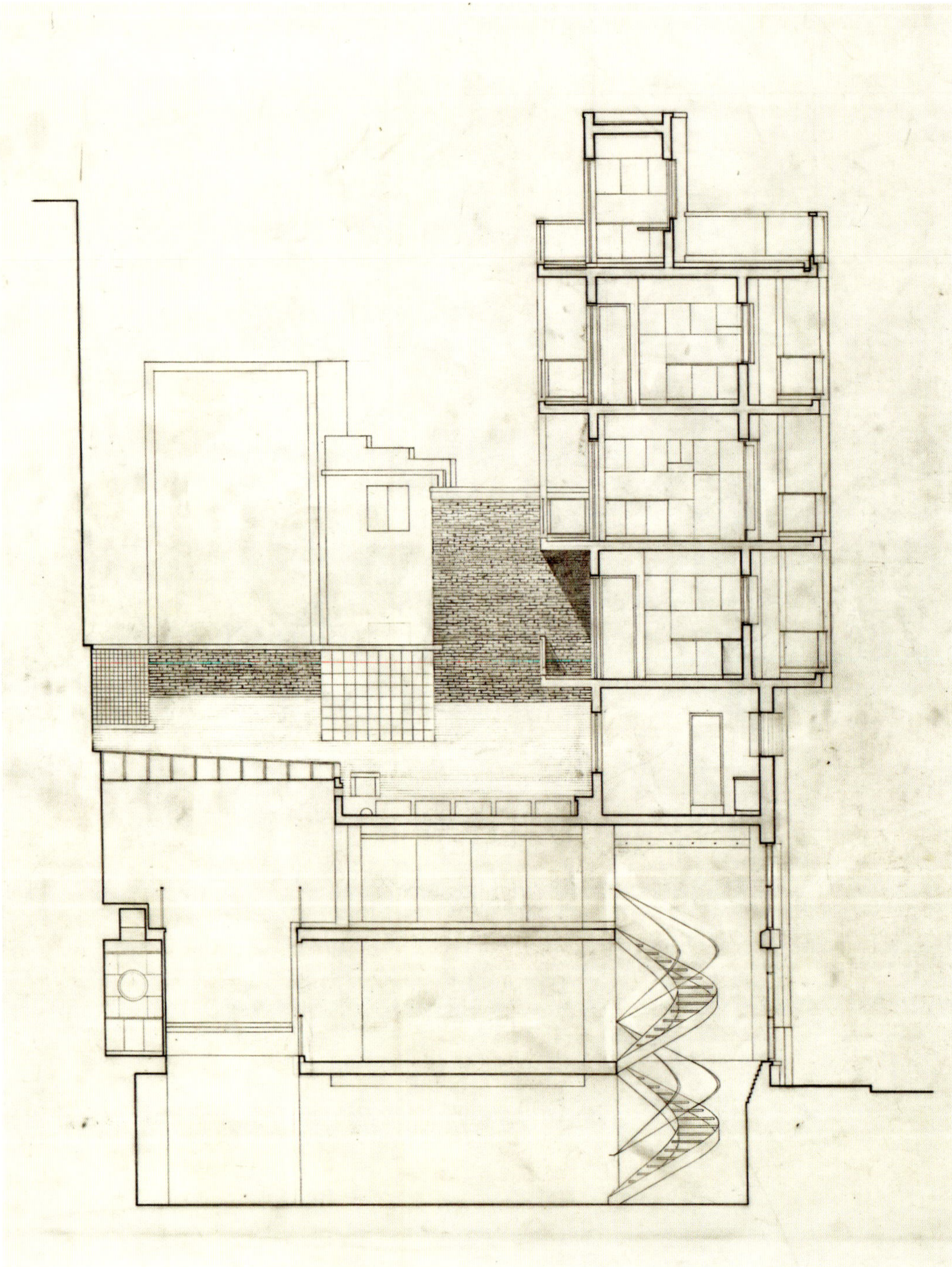

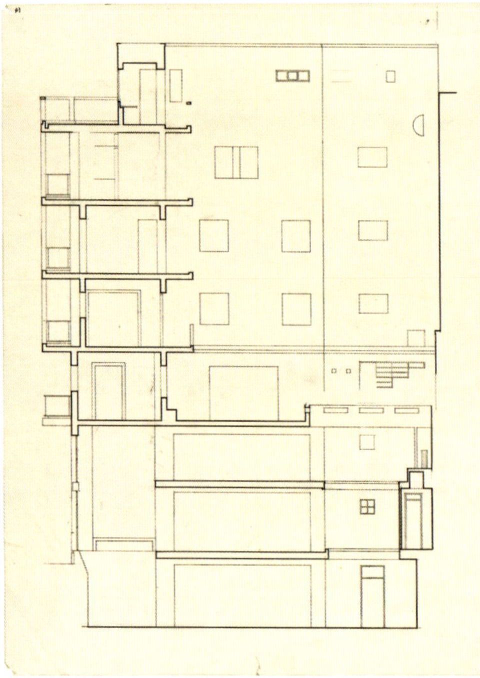

Clockwise from left: building section facing south; building section facing north; sections facing west through atrium

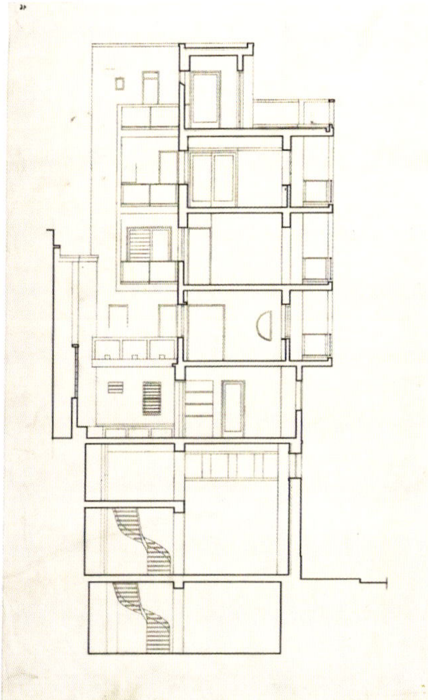

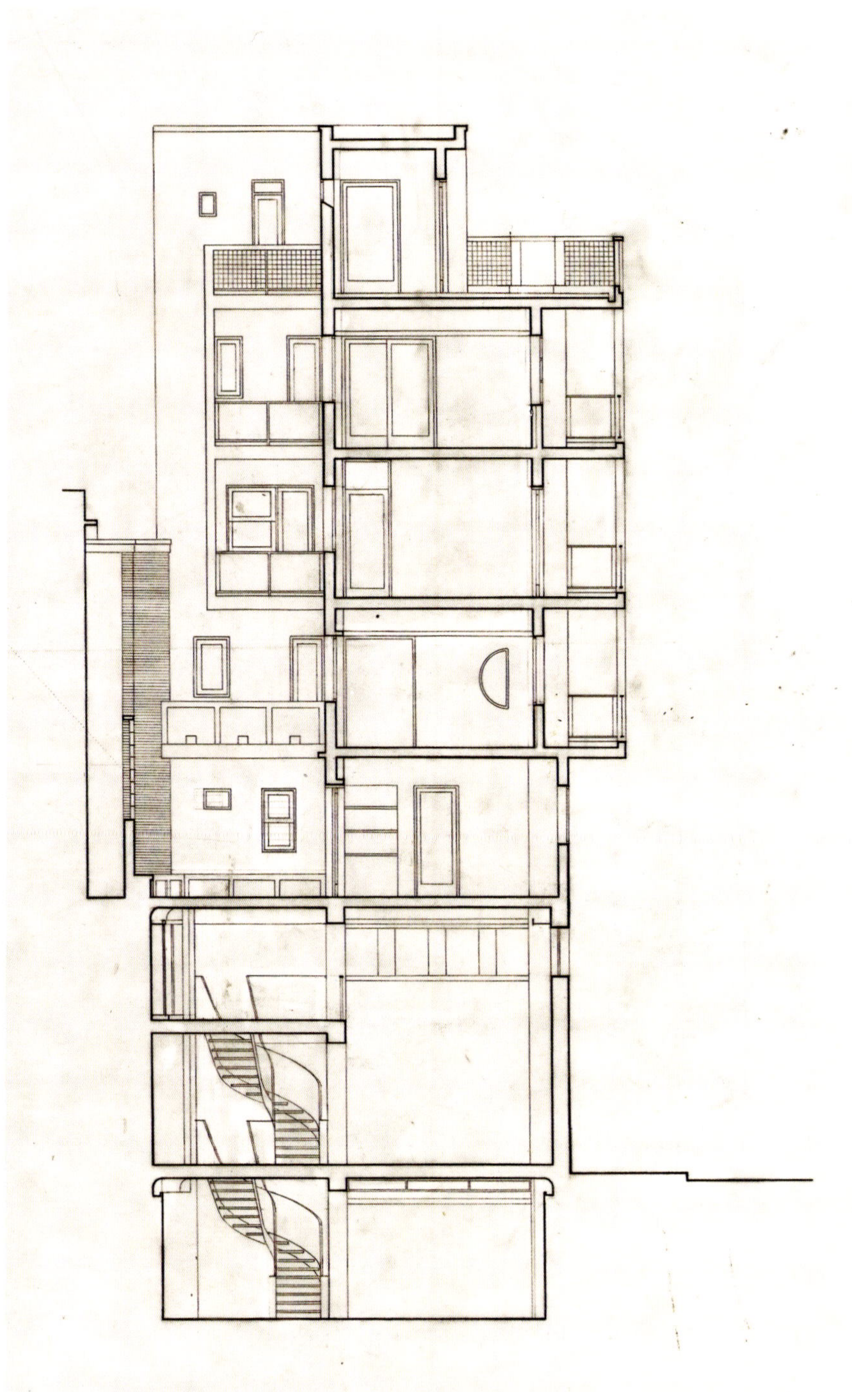

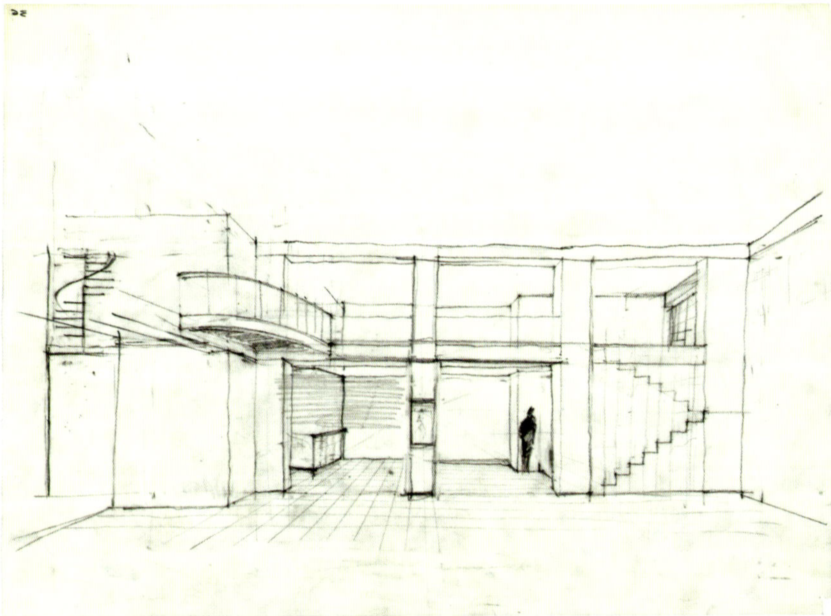

This page: sketches of main gallery and mezzanine interiors
Opposite page (l-r): partial section facing south atrium wall; partial section facing south through gallery spaces

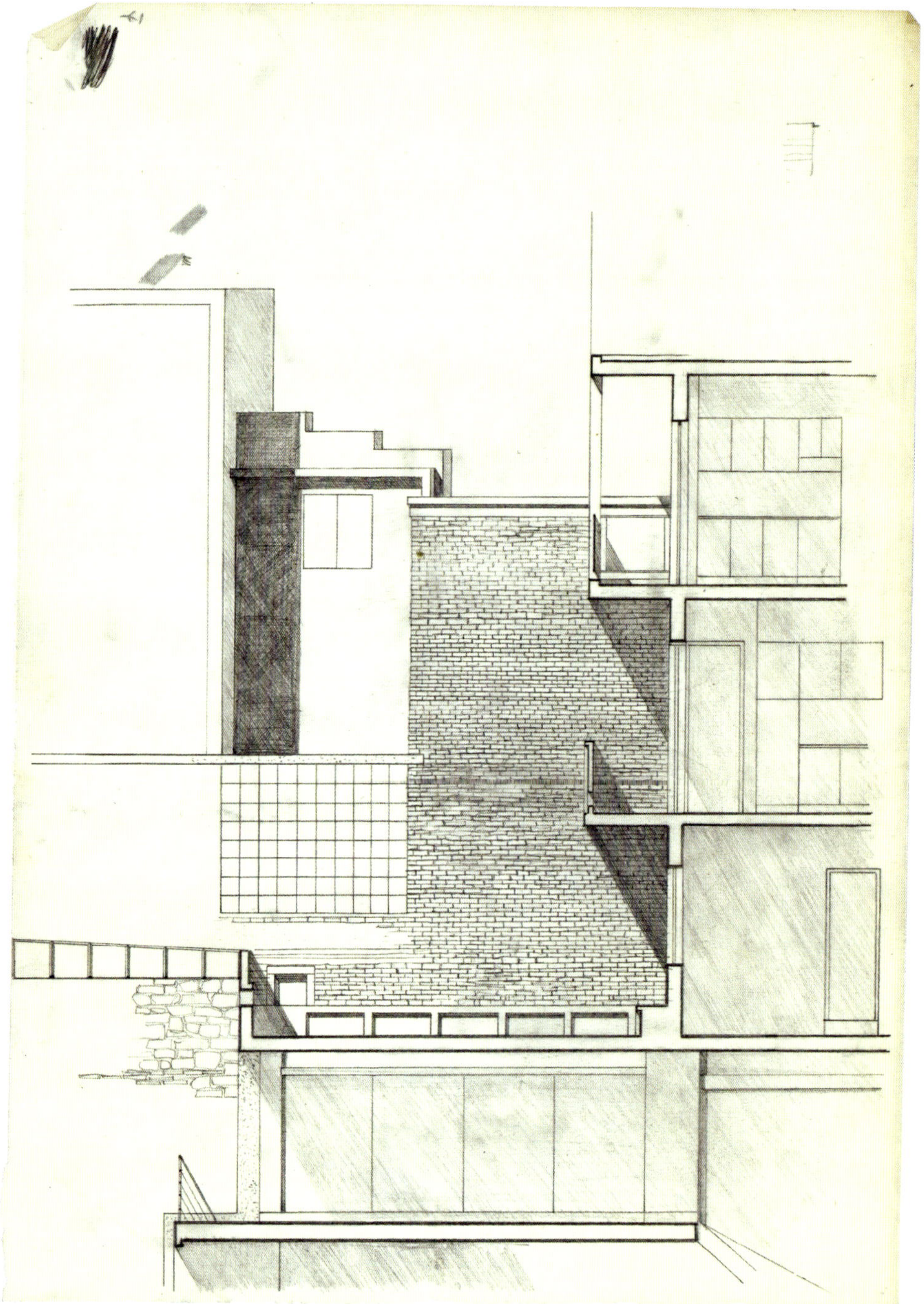

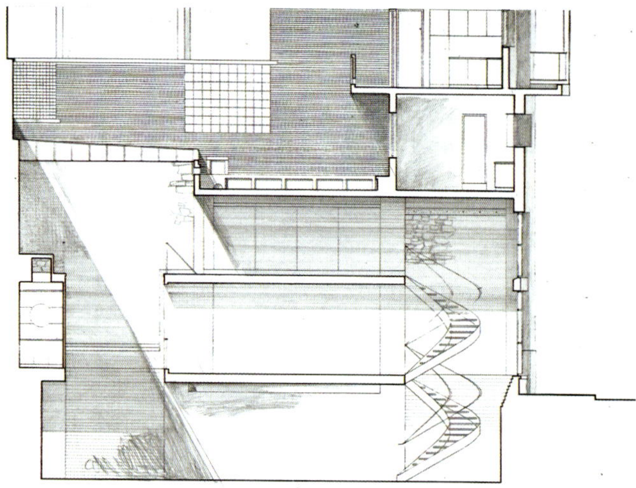

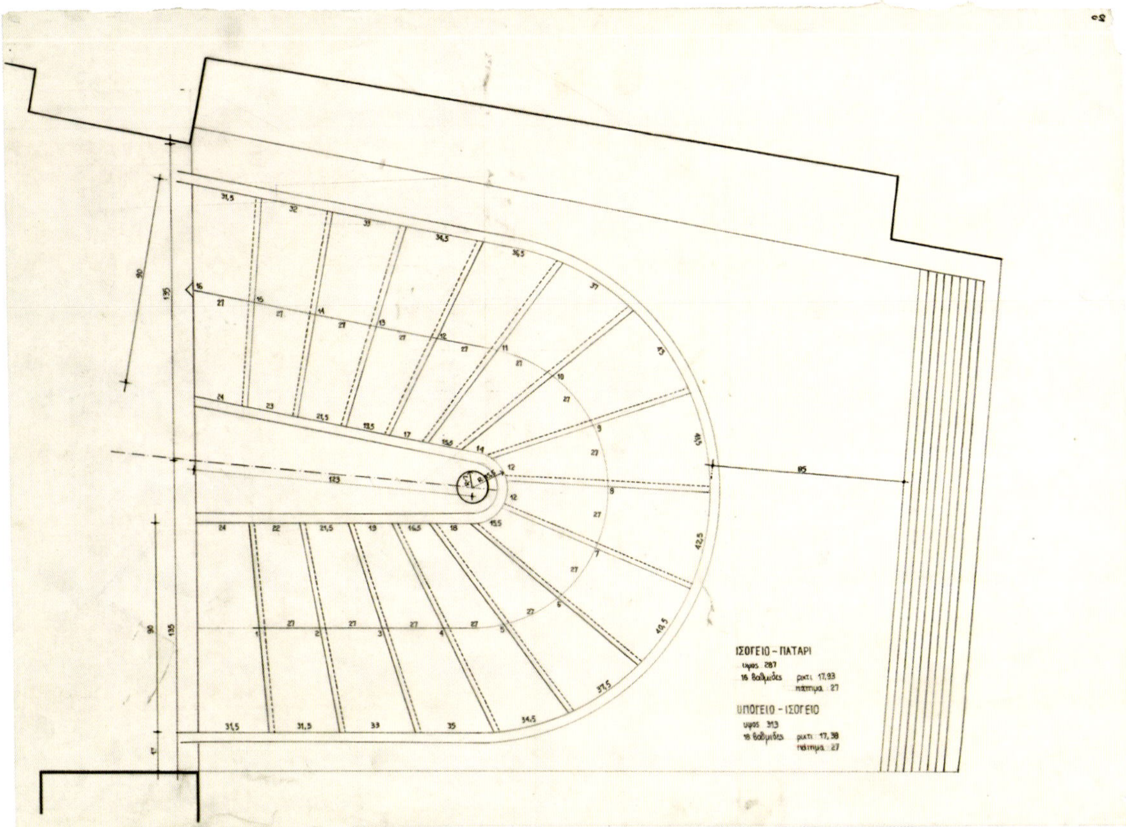

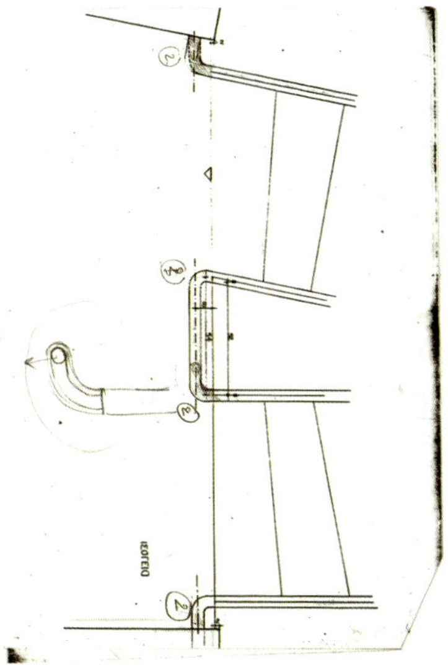

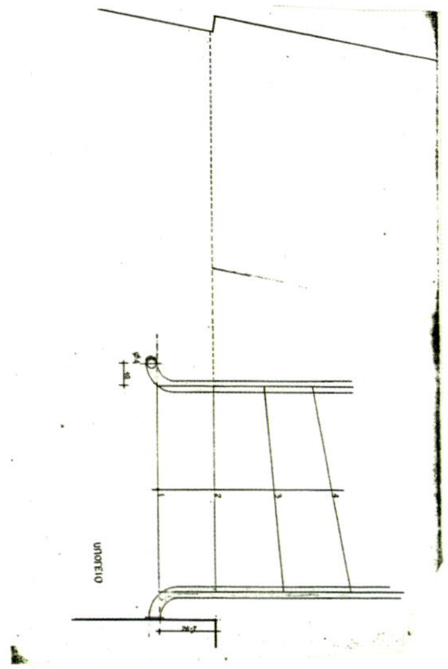

This page: plan and details of metal staircase in galleries
Opposite page (l-r): side view of metal staircase; front view of metal staircase

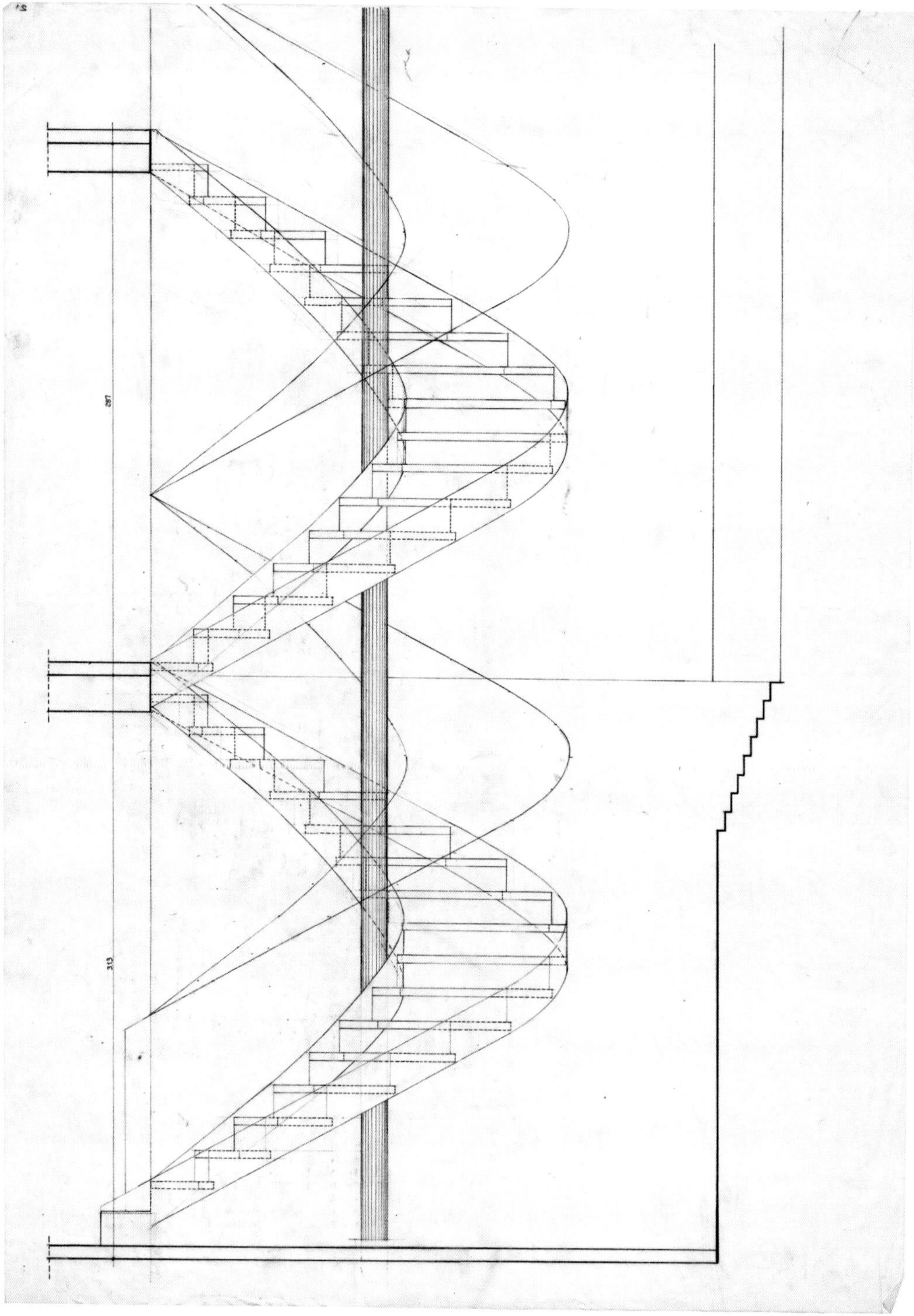

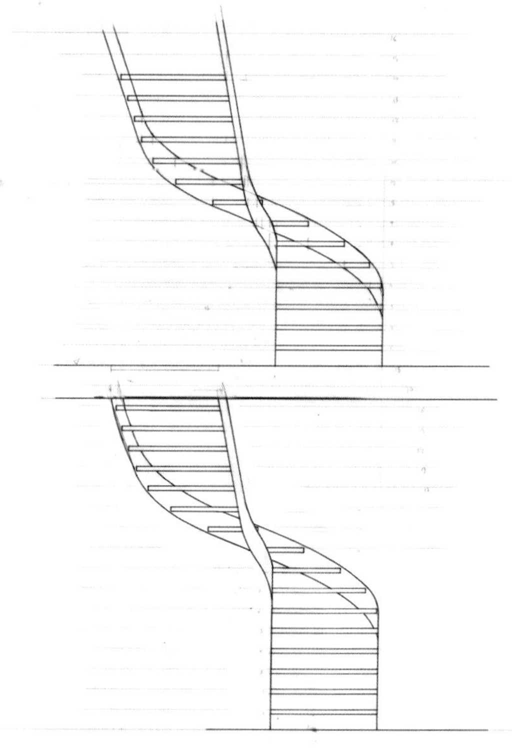

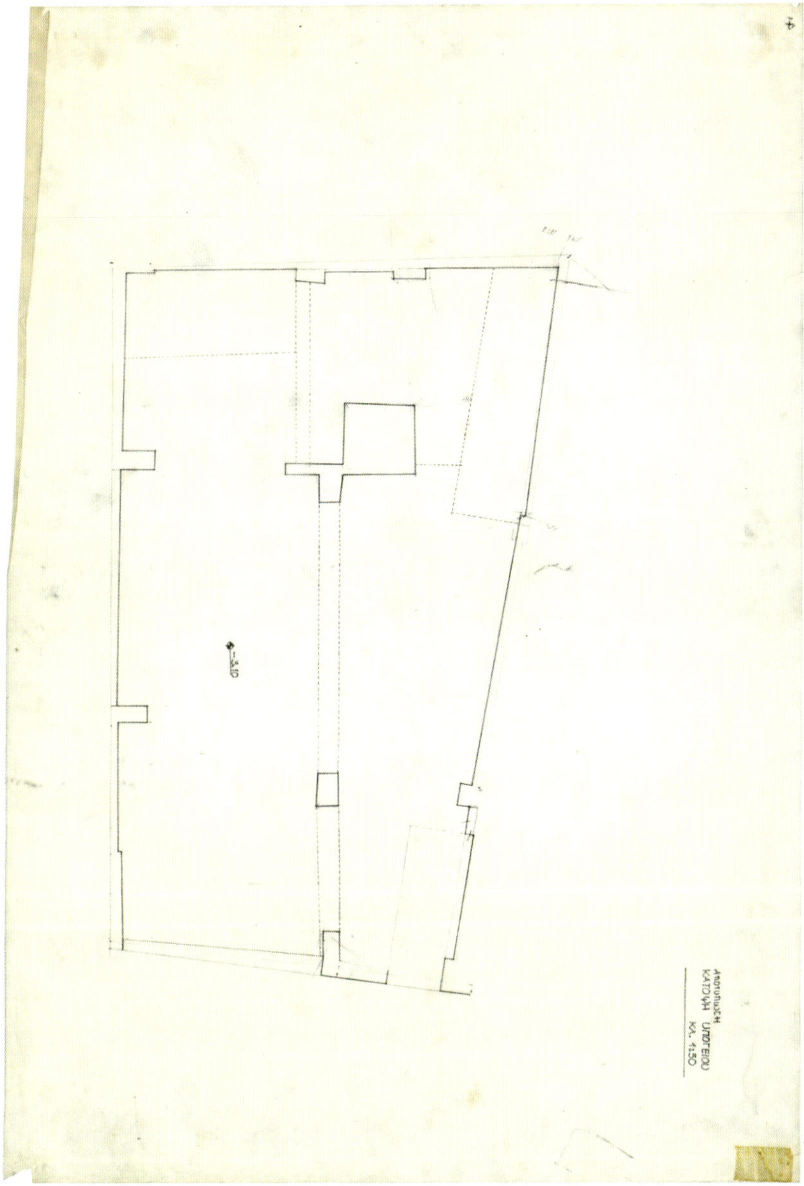

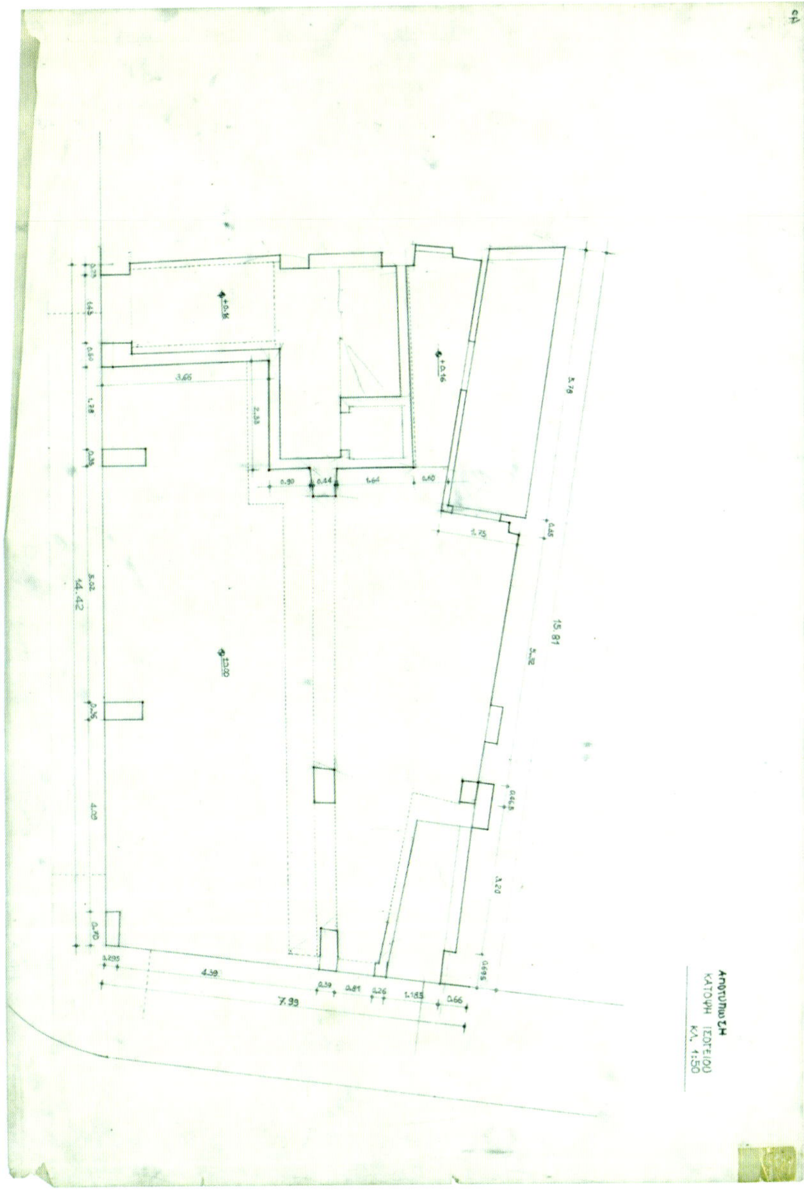

Above left: existing basement plan, 1990
Above: existing ground floor plan, 1990

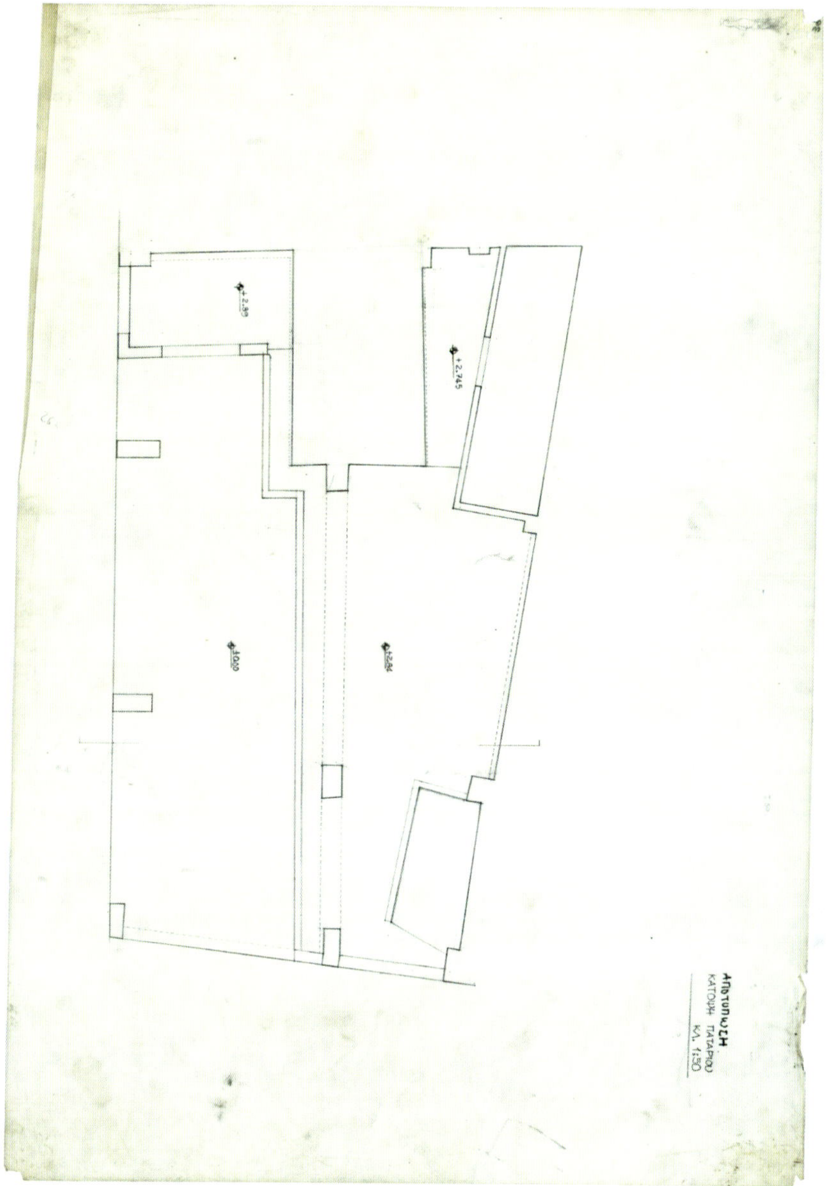

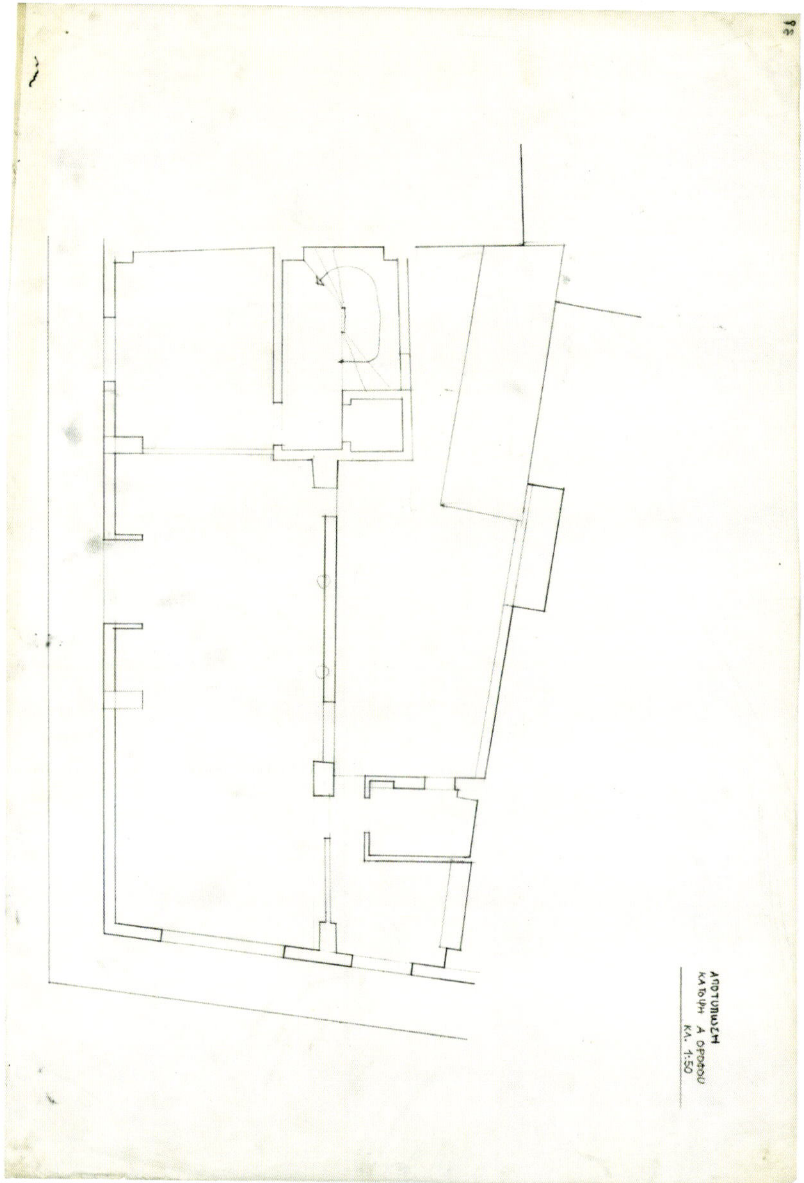

Above: existing mezzanine plan, 1990
Right: existing first floor plan, 1990

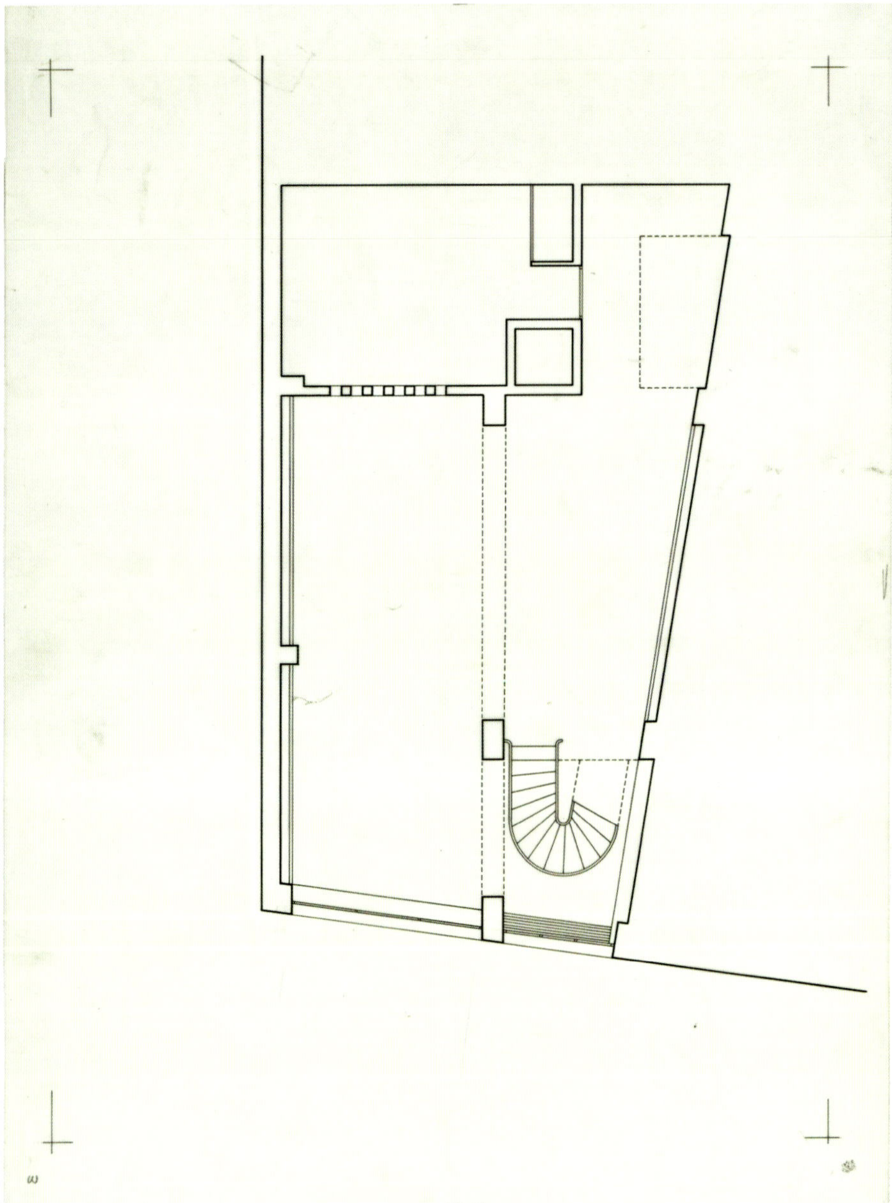

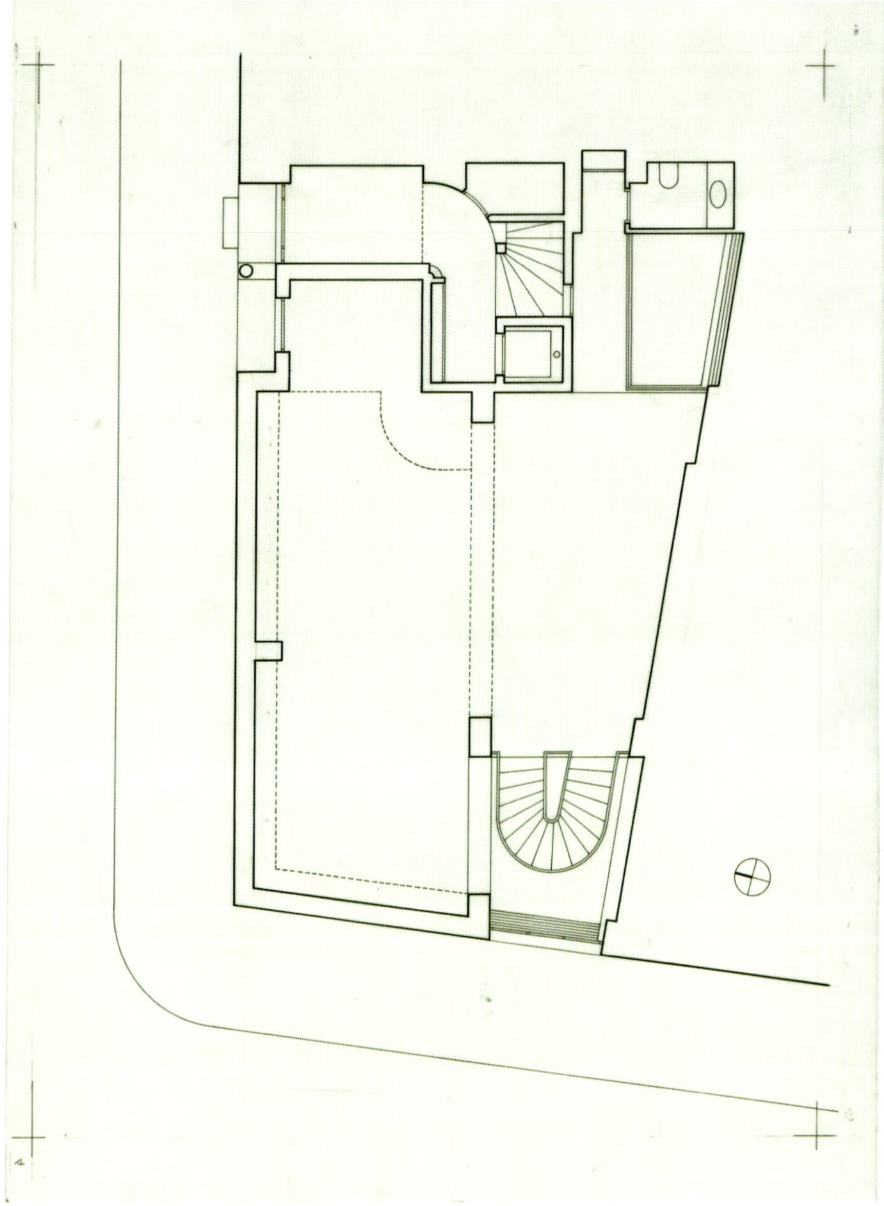

Above left: basement plan as constructed
Above: ground floor plan as constructed

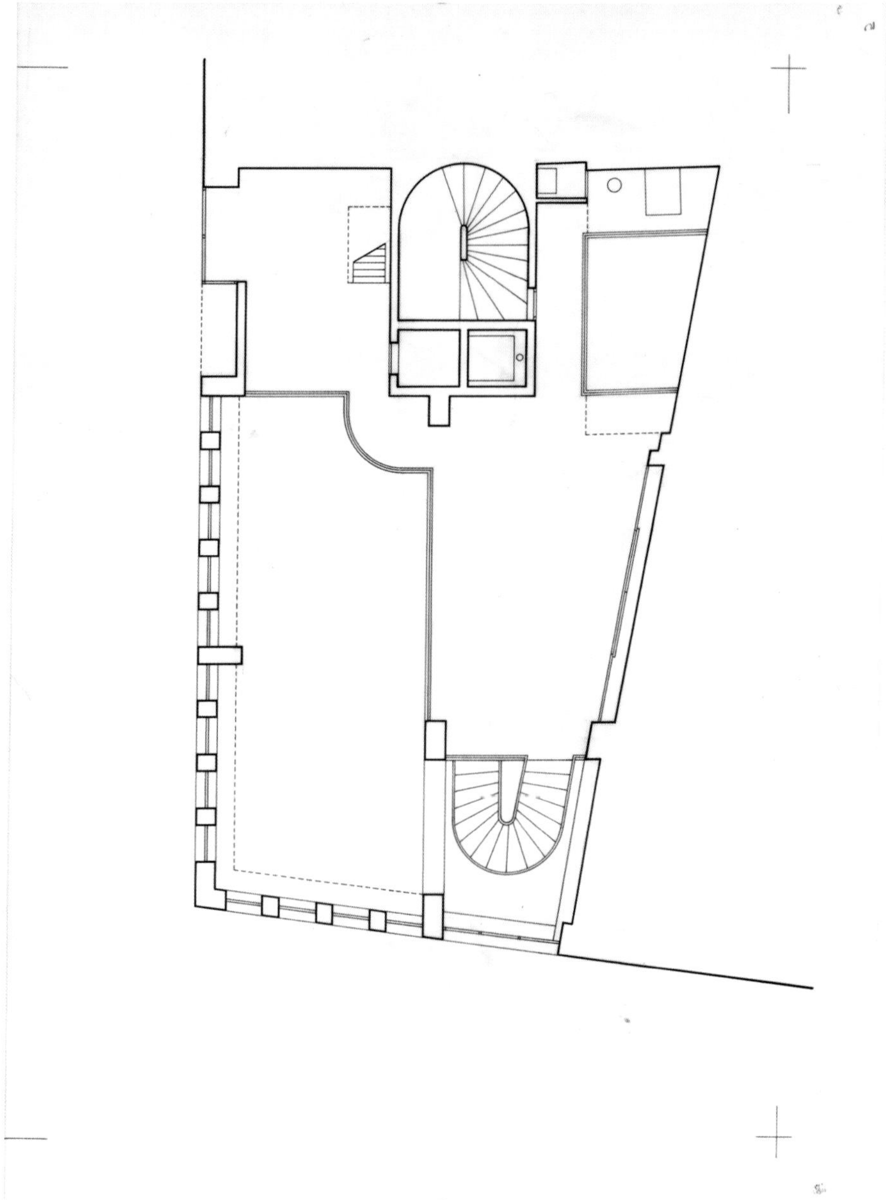

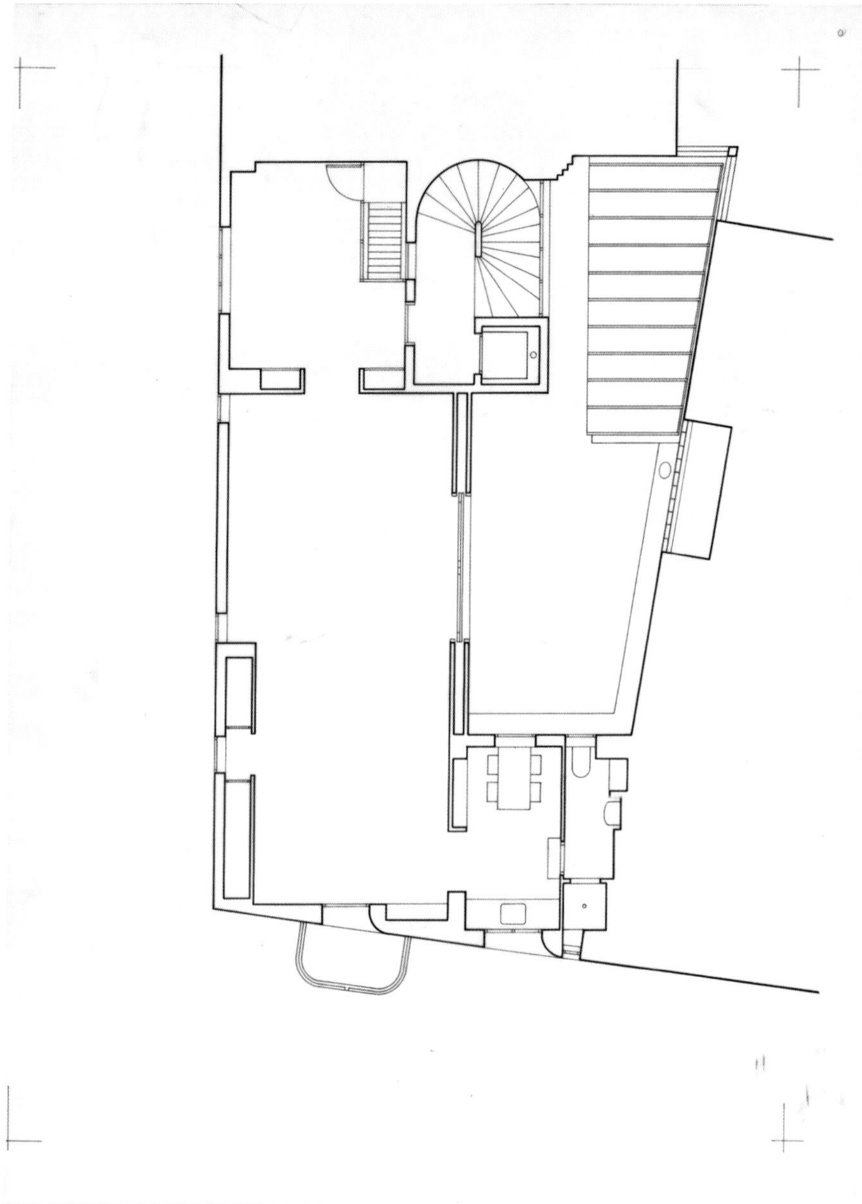

Above: mezzanine plan as constructed
Above right: first floor plan as constructed

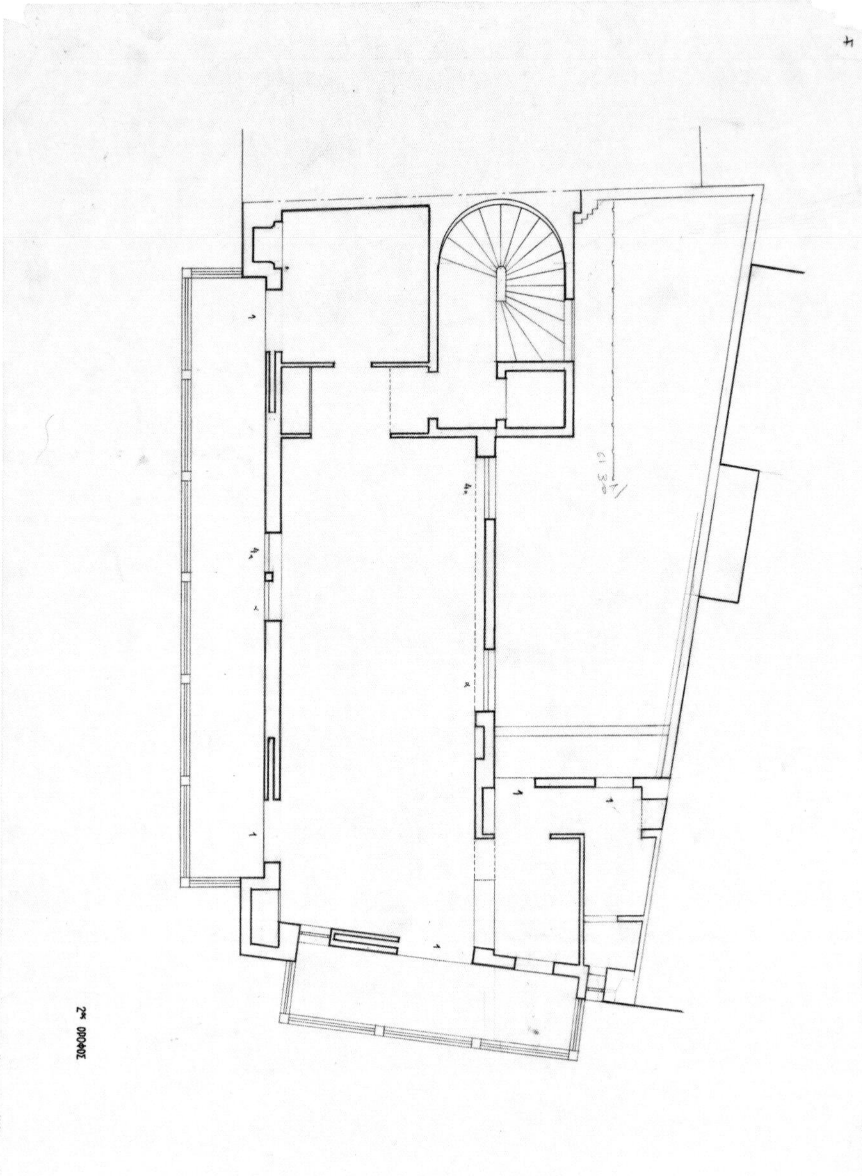

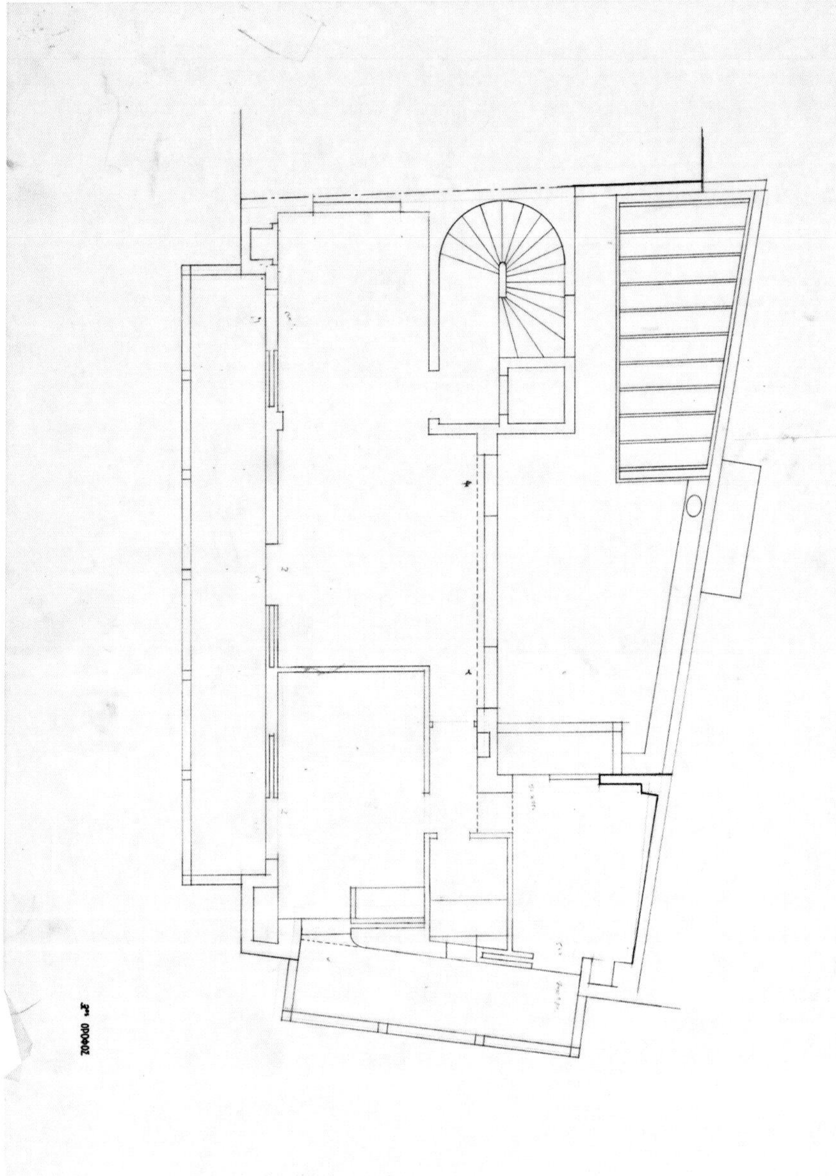

Above left: second floor plan as constructed
Above: third floor plan as constructed

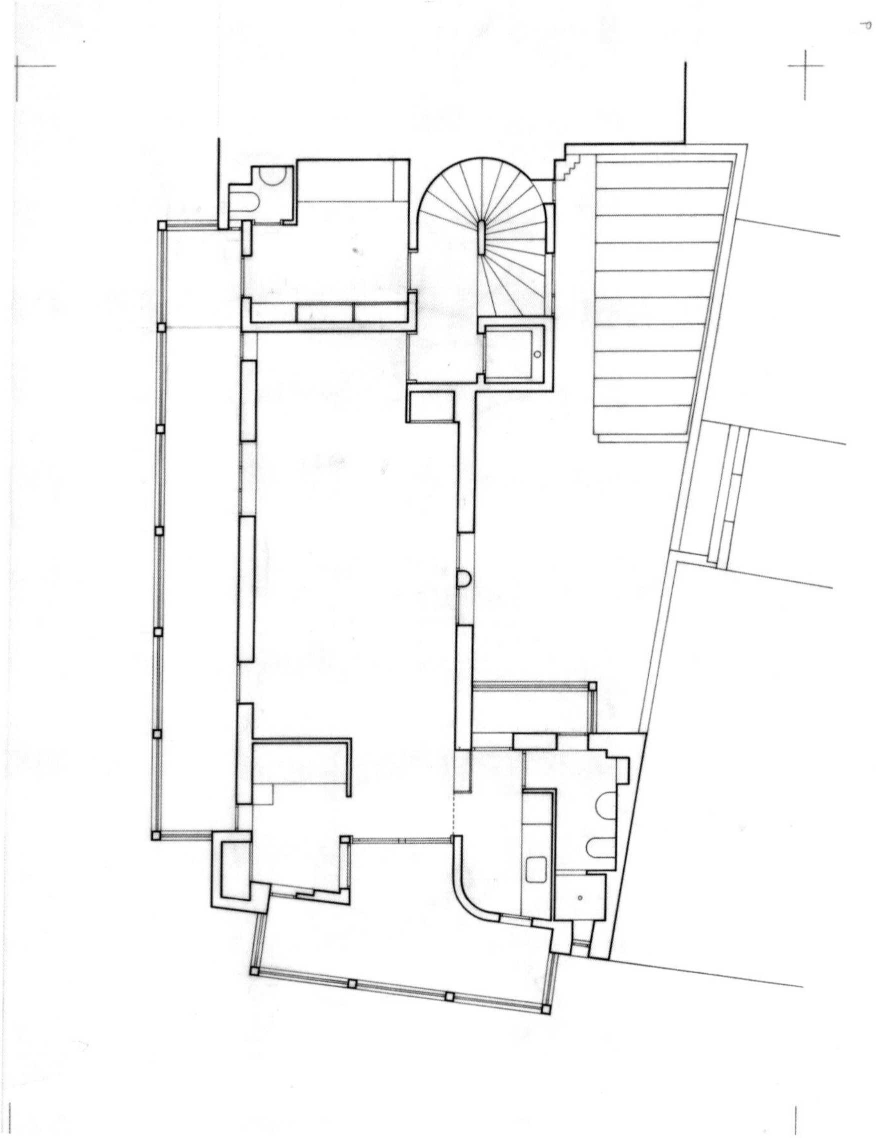

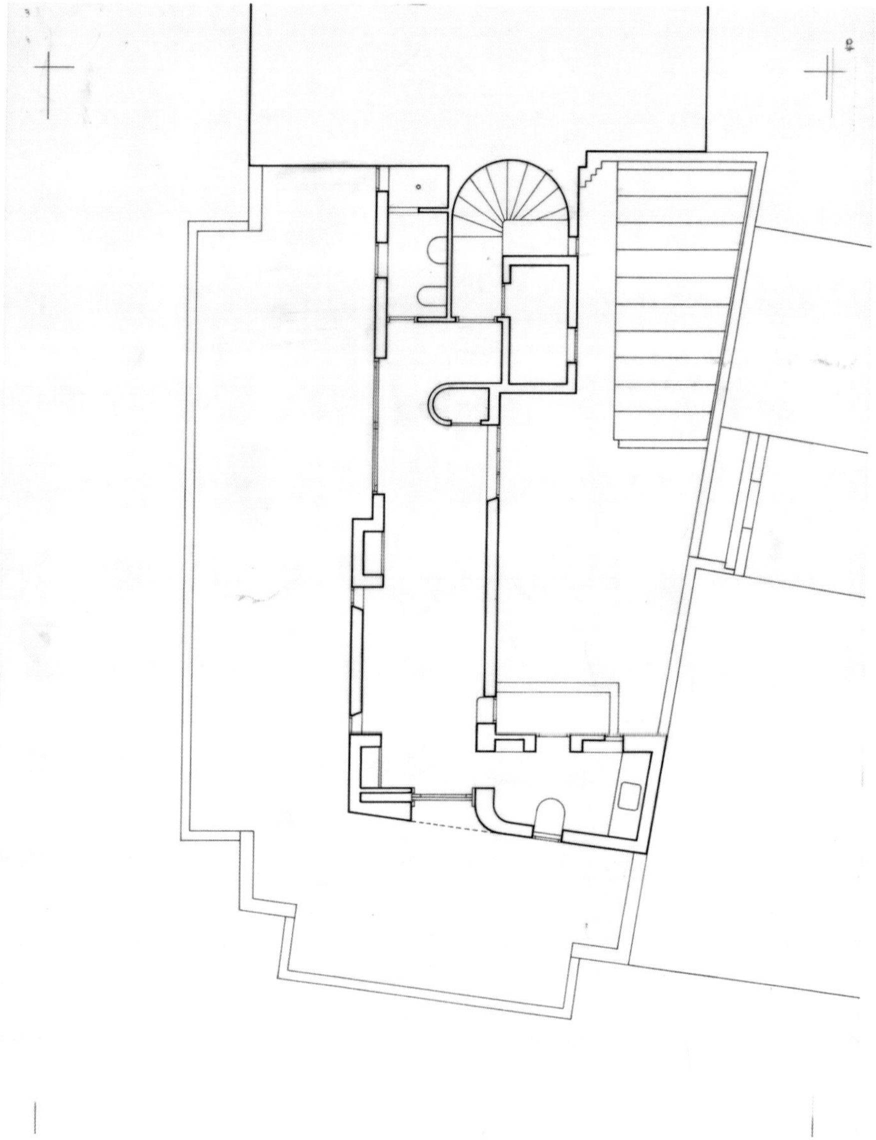

Above: Fourth floor plan as constructed
Above right: roof terrace plan as constructed

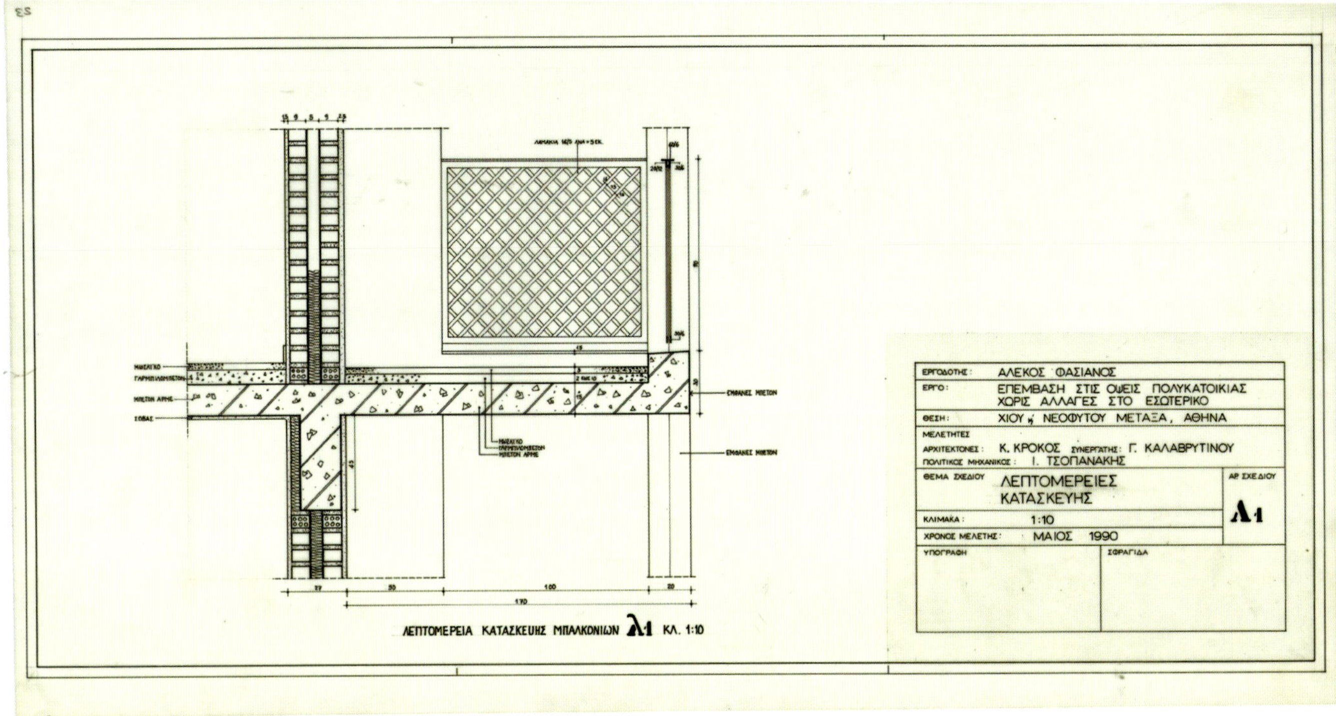

Above: typical building section, 1990, not to scale
Oppositie page: diagrammatic plans and sections of the building, 1990, not to scale

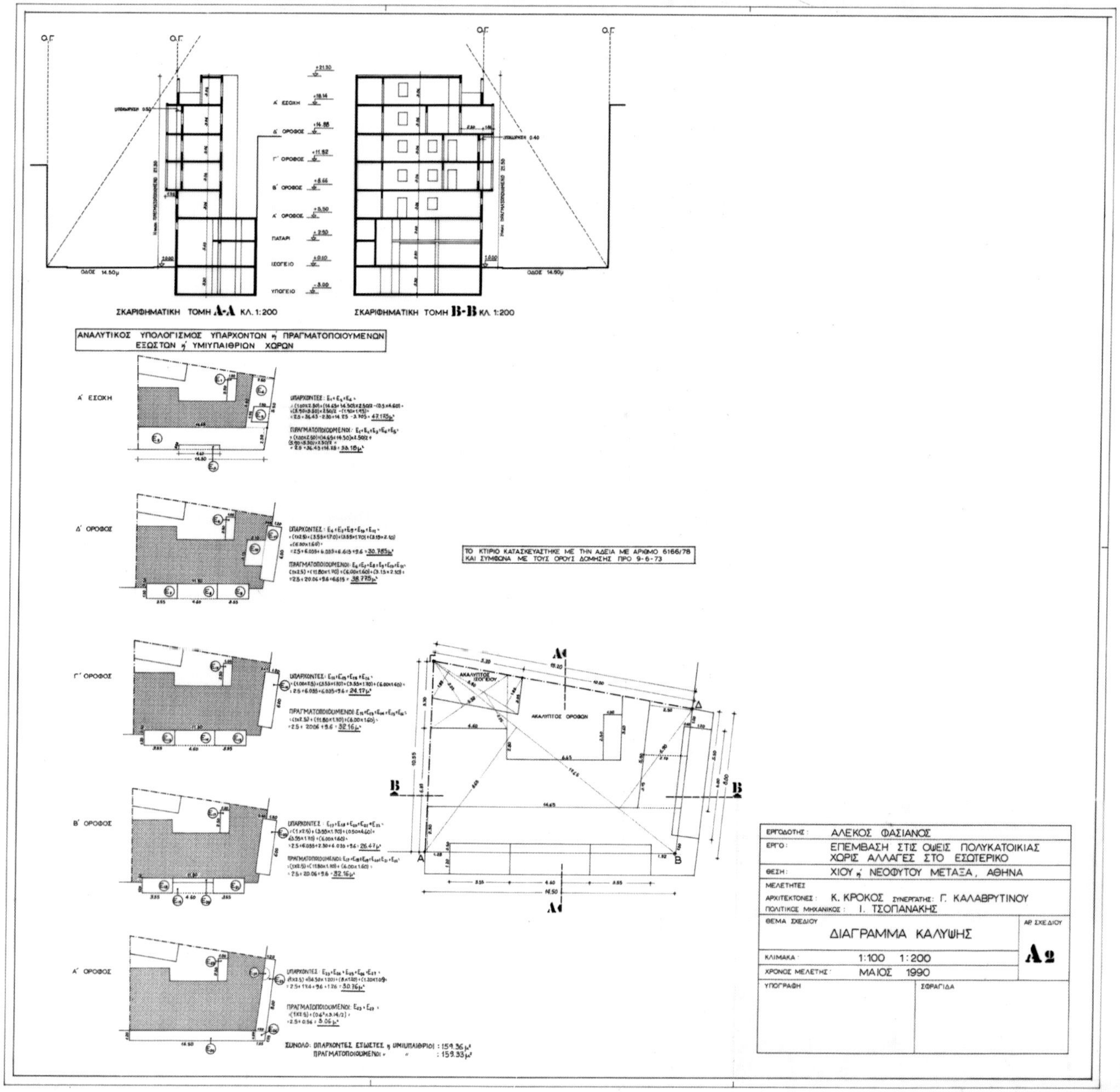

ΣΚΑΡΙΦΗΜΑΤΙΚΗ ΤΟΜΗ Α-Α ΚΛ. 1:200
ΣΚΑΡΙΦΗΜΑΤΙΚΗ ΤΟΜΗ Β-Β ΚΛ. 1:200
ΑΝΑΛΥΤΙΚΟΣ ΥΠΟΛΟΓΙΣΜΟΣ ΥΠΑΡΧΟΝΤΩΝ ή ΠΡΑΓΜΑΤΟΠΟΙΟΥΜΕΝΩΝ ΕΞΩΣΤΩΝ ή ΥΜΙΥΠΑΙΘΡΙΩΝ ΧΩΡΩΝ
Α΄ ΕΣΟΧΗ
Δ΄ ΟΡΟΦΟΣ
Γ΄ ΟΡΟΦΟΣ
Β΄ ΟΡΟΦΟΣ
Α΄ ΟΡΟΦΟΣ
ΤΟ ΚΤΙΡΙΟ ΚΑΤΑΣΚΕΥΑΣΤΗΚΕ ΜΕ ΤΗΝ ΑΔΕΙΑ ΜΕ ΑΡΙΘΜΟ 6166/78 ΚΑΙ ΣΥΜΦΩΝΑ ΜΕ ΤΟΥΣ ΟΡΟΥΣ ΔΟΜΗΣΗΣ ΠΡΟ 9-6-73
ΕΡΓΟΔΟΤΗΣ: ΑΛΕΚΟΣ ΦΑΣΙΑΝΟΣ
ΕΡΓΟ: ΕΠΕΜΒΑΣΗ ΣΤΙΣ ΟΨΕΙΣ ΠΟΛΥΚΑΤΟΙΚΙΑΣ ΧΩΡΙΣ ΑΛΛΑΓΕΣ ΣΤΟ ΕΣΩΤΕΡΙΚΟ
ΘΕΣΗ: ΧΙΟΥ ή ΝΕΟΦΥΤΟΥ ΜΕΤΑΞΑ, ΑΘΗΝΑ
ΜΕΛΕΤΗΤΕΣ
ΑΡΧΙΤΕΚΤΟΝΕΣ: Κ. ΚΡΟΚΟΣ ΣΥΝΕΡΓΑΤΗΣ: Γ. ΚΑΛΑΒΡΥΤΙΝΟΥ
ΠΟΛΙΤΙΚΟΣ ΜΗΧΑΝΙΚΟΣ: Ι. ΤΣΟΠΑΝΑΚΗΣ
ΘΕΜΑ ΣΧΕΔΙΟΥ
ΔΙΑΓΡΑΜΜΑ ΚΑΛΥΨΗΣ
ΑΡ. ΣΧΕΔΙΟΥ
Α2
ΚΛΙΜΑΚΑ: 1:100 1:200
ΧΡΟΝΟΣ ΜΕΛΕΤΗΣ: ΜΑΙΟΣ 1990
ΥΠΟΓΡΑΦΗ
ΣΦΡΑΓΙΔΑ

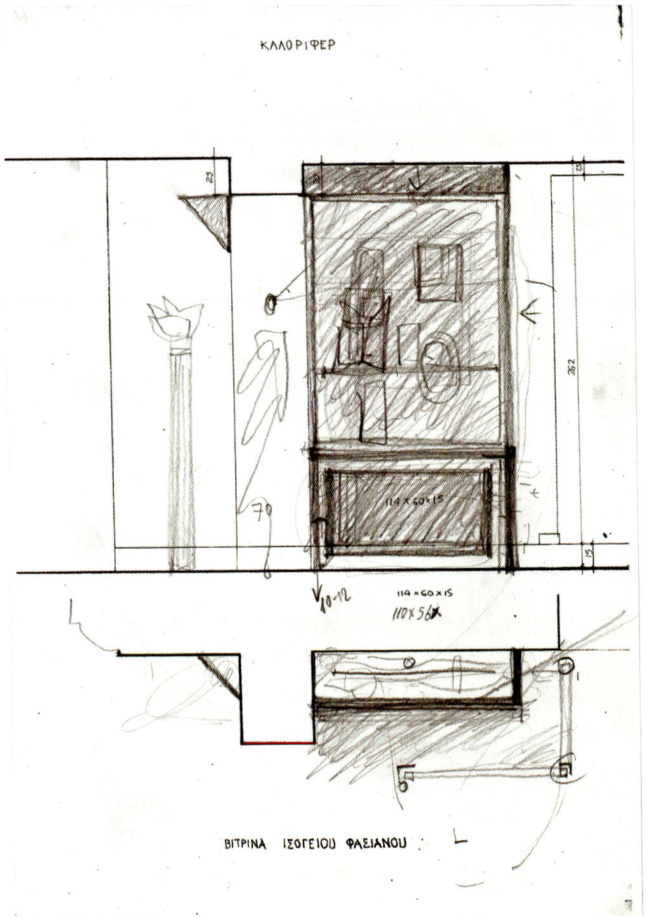

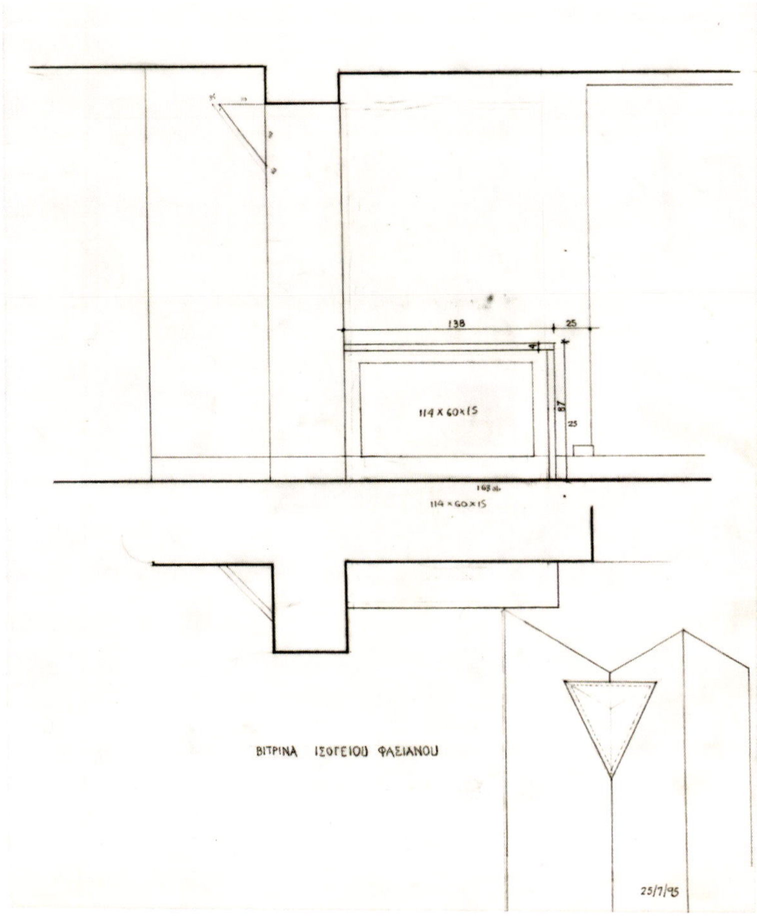

Above left: sketch for unrealized ground floor gallery decorative column and vitrine
Above: ground floor gallery lighting and radiator details; *Opposite page, clockwise from top left:* drawing for gallery entrance door; plan and elevation of unrealized gallery reception; apartment building and gallery entrance door

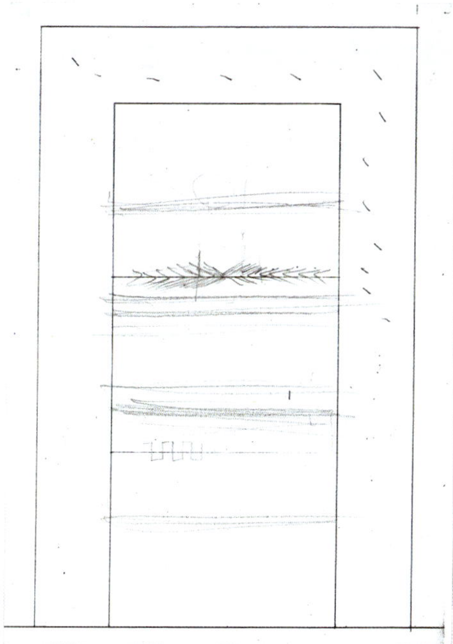

ΣΧ 1
ΚΛ. 1:20

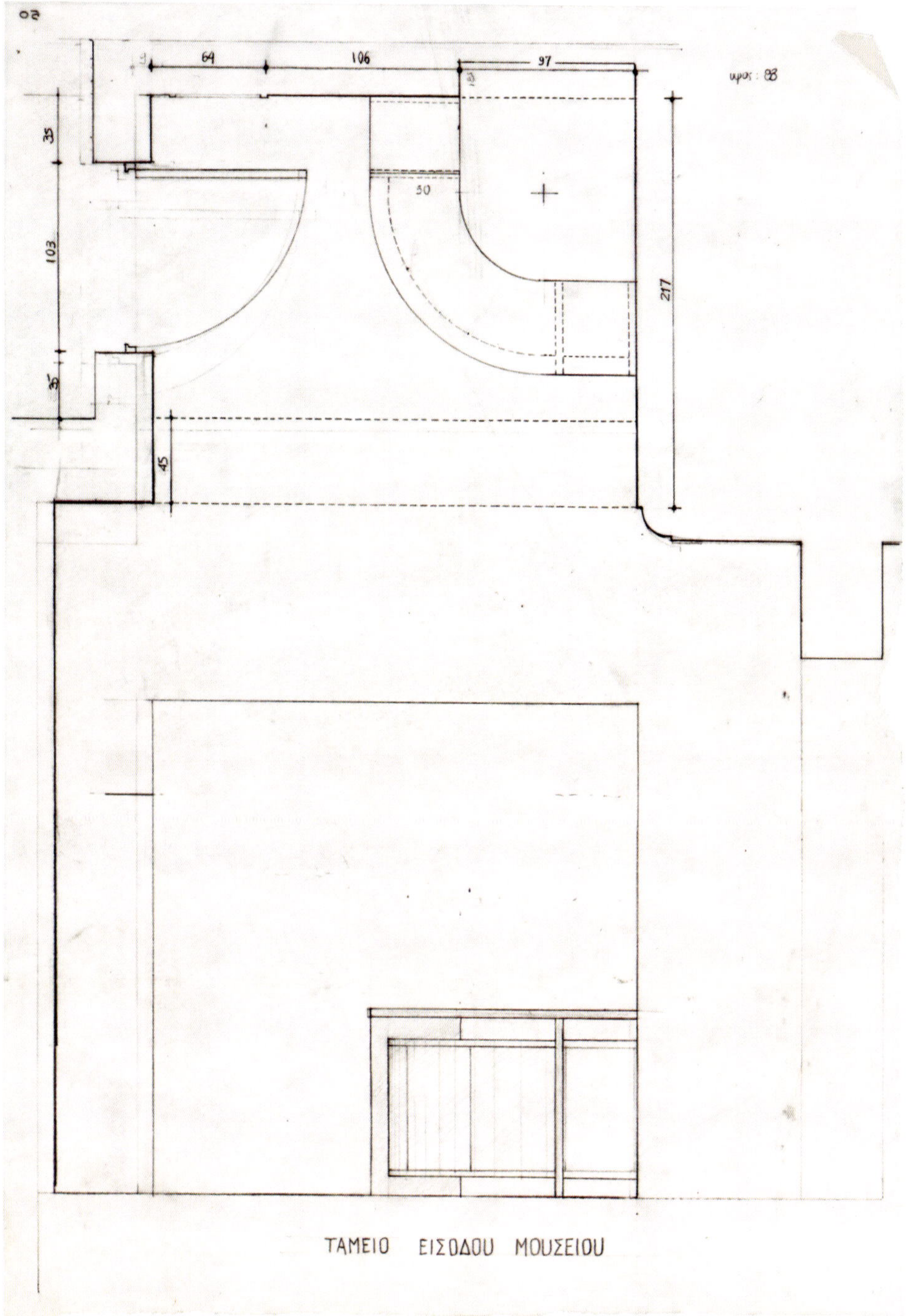
64
106
97
35
103
217
45
50
ΤΑΜΕΙΟ ΕΙΣΟΔΟΥ ΜΟΥΣΕΙΟΥ

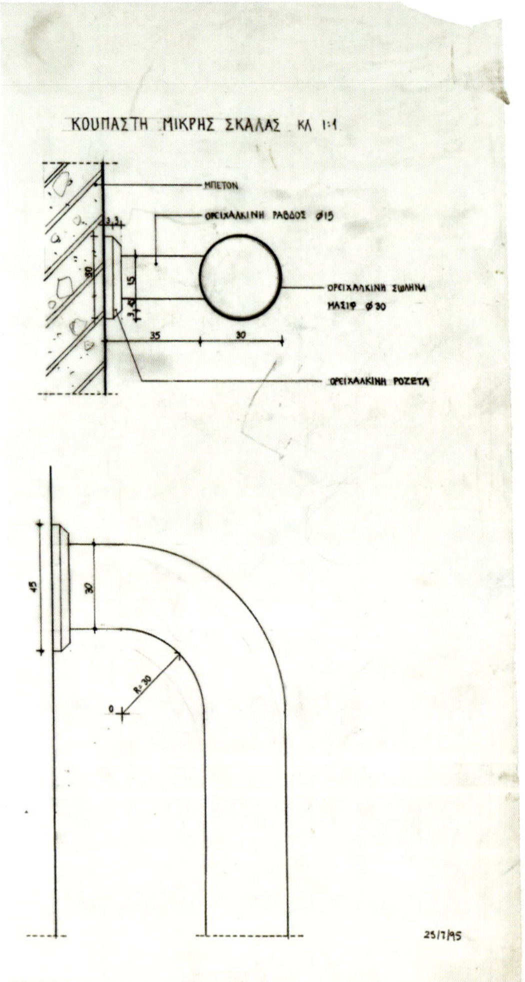
ΚΟΥΠΑΣΤΗ ΜΙΚΡΗΣ ΣΚΑΛΑΣ ΚΛ 1:1
ΜΠΕΤΟΝ
ΟΡΕΙΧΑΛΚΙΝΗ ΡΑΒΔΟΣ Ø15
ΟΡΕΙΧΑΛΚΙΝΗ ΣΩΛΗΝΑ ΜΑΣΙΦ Ø30
ΟΡΕΙΧΑΛΚΙΝΗ ΡΟΖΕΤΑ
25/7/95

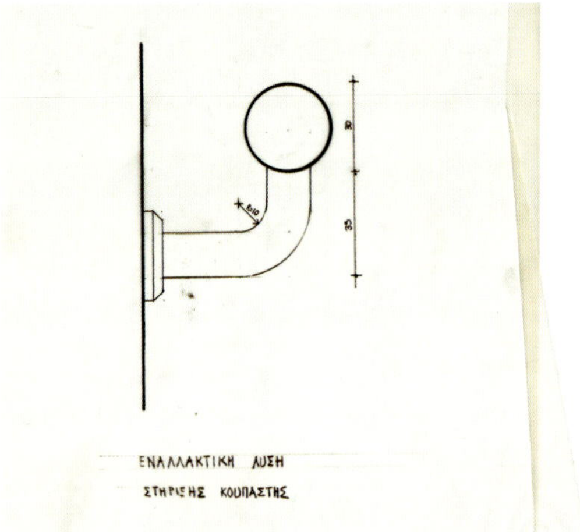
ΕΝΑΛΛΑΚΤΙΚΗ ΛΥΣΗ
ΣΤΗΡΙΞΗΣ ΚΟΥΠΑΣΤΗΣ

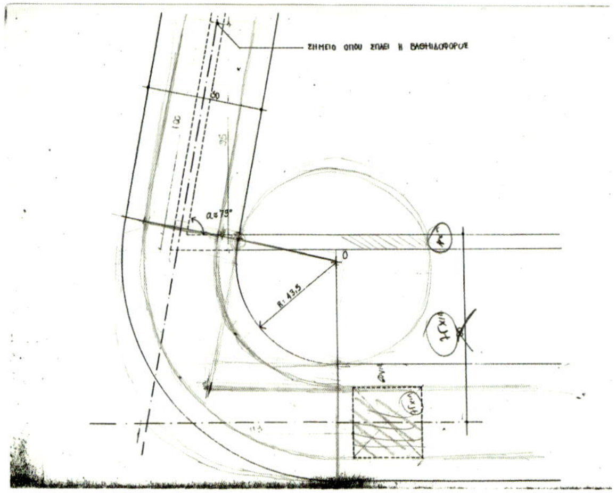
ΣΗΜΕΙΟ ΟΠΟΥ ΣΠΑΕΙ Η ΒΑΘΜΙΔΟΦΟΡΟΣ

Opposite page, clockwise from left: drawings for small staircase hand railing, detail of main metal staircase
Right: sketch for decorative column on mezzanine level, bearing sculpture by Alekos Fassianos

KOUZINA 1ου
ΑΠΟΡΡΟΦΗΤ
97.50
60.00
3.00
59.50
179.50

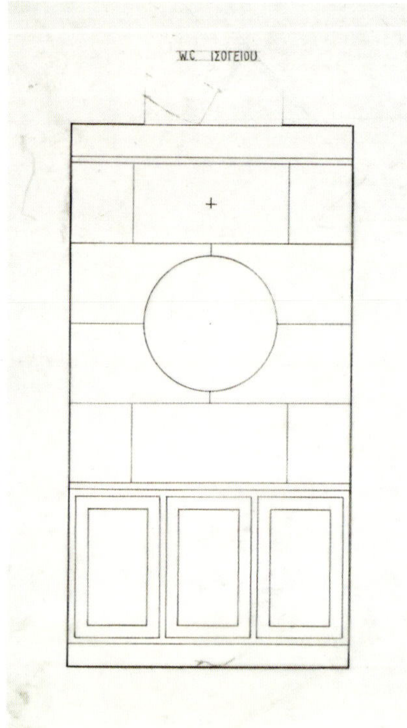
W.C. ΙΣΟΓΕΙΟΥ

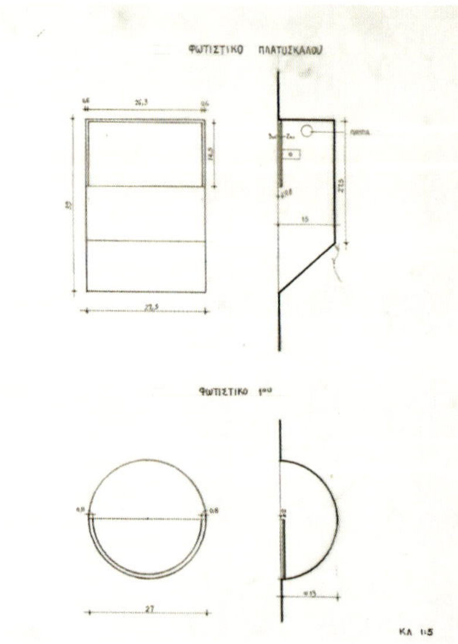
ΦΩΤΙΣΤΙΚΟ ΠΛΑΤΥΣΚΑΛΟΥ
ΦΩΤΙΣΤΙΚΟ 1ου
ΚΑ 1:5

Above: balcony door details; *Right:* kitchen cupboard drawing
Opposite page, clockwise from far left: fourth floor kitchen cupboards, drawing of ground floor WC wall; staircase landing wall lighting fittings

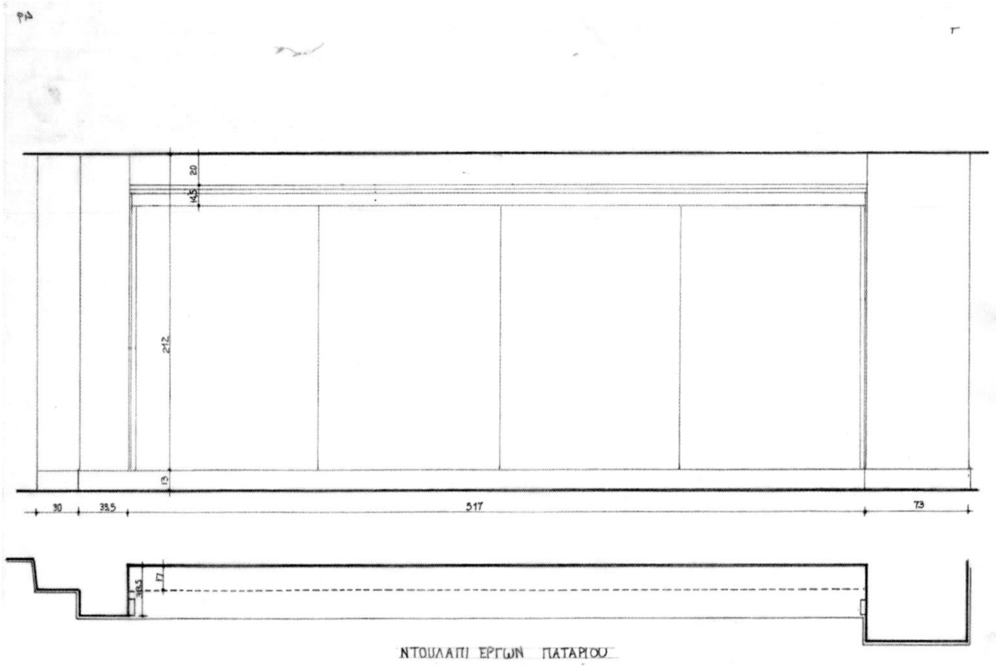

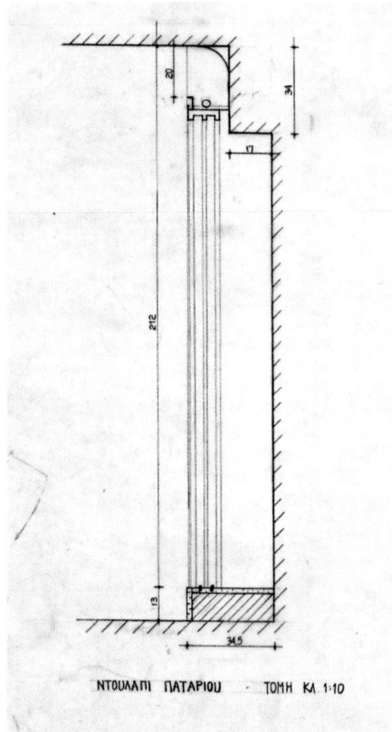

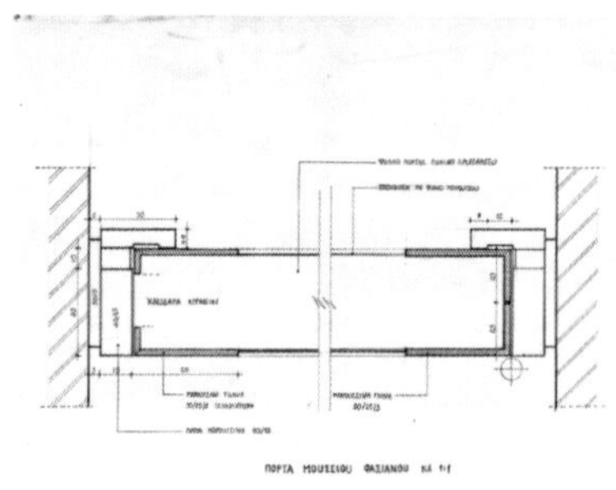

Clockwise, from above: elevation and plan of mezzanine wall; section of mezzanine storage cupboard for paintings; gallery entrance door detail; *Opposite clockwise, from above:* radiator cover details; interior details; frame details

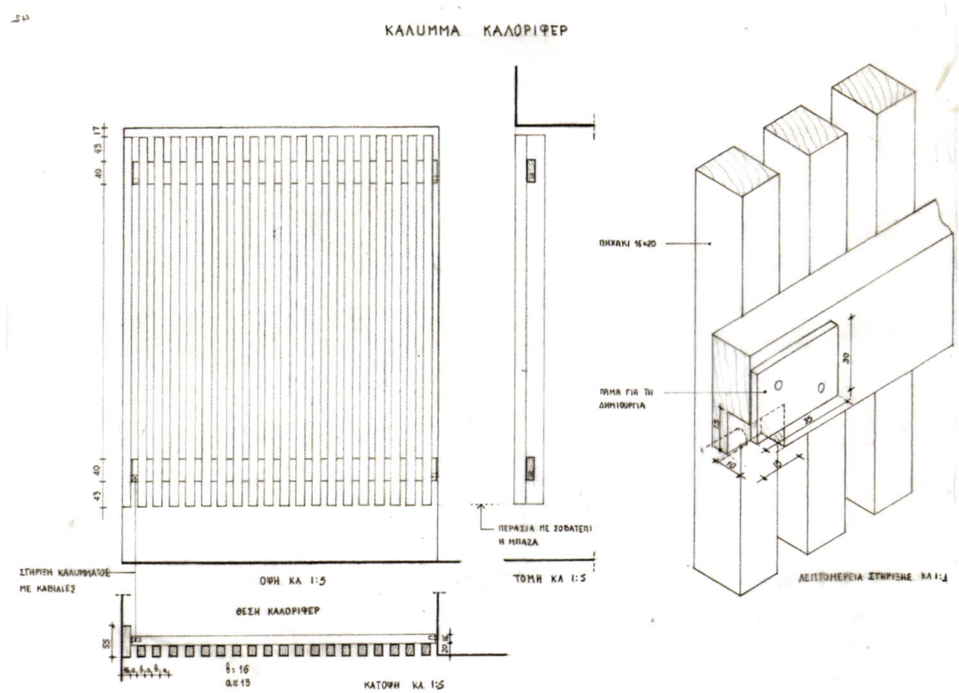
ΚΑΛΥΜΜΑ ΚΑΛΟΡΙΦΕΡ
ΠΗΧΑΚΙ 16×20
ΓΑΜΑ ΓΙΑ ΤΗ
ΔΗΜΙΟΥΡΓΙΑ
ΠΕΡΑΣΙΑ ΜΕ ΣΟΒΑΤΕΠΙ
Η ΜΠΑΖΑ
ΣΤΗΡΙΞΗ ΚΑΛΥΜΜΑΤΟΣ
ΜΕ ΚΑΒΙΛΙΕΣ
ΟΨΗ ΚΑ 1:5
ΤΟΜΗ ΚΑ 1:5
ΛΕΠΤΟΜΕΡΕΙΑ ΣΤΗΡΙΞΗΣ ΚΑ 1:1
ΘΕΣΗ ΚΑΛΟΡΙΦΕΡ
ΚΑΤΟΨΗ ΚΑ 1:5

Kyriakos Krokos, *Folk Palace*, crayons

An Architecture of Serenity

Elias Constantopoulos

The Metamorphosis of Space Through Light and Matter

"How from nothing the primal thing arose,
How power of light through the night did ring,
Imbuing the depths of the beings all;
Thus welled up desiring's surge.
And the elements disclosed themselves,
With hunger into one another poured,
'All-imbuing, all-imbued'
...And rolling up and down did go
The all and one eternal thing,
'Ever changing, ever constant!'"
— Johann Wolfgang von Goethe[1]

When writing a short history of the contemporary Greek apartment block,[2] noting a shift from the post war development of a typical form of urban residence, towards the a-typical agglomerations of the 1980s, I found myself at an impasse trying to carry the story through to the last two decades of the century. The cityscape was mute, laden with endless, more or less unnoticeable repetitions of the balconied form, which express the status of horizontal ownership that has been the mark of the modern Greek city. The merits of the apartment block typology have been noted by critics such as Kenneth Frampton,[3] but still these buildings present many unresolved problems—social, aesthetic and functional—in terms of their lack of surrounding public space, inadequate lighting and ventilating conditions, parking facilities, and other problems.

Although I felt somewhat uneasy about how to end the essay, a vivid, recurring picture in my mind came to the rescue. This was the image of the open space atrium (*aithrion*) of the Fassianos building designed by Kyriakos Krokos in Athens, which I had recently visited. Here, as required by law, Krokos had salvaged the outdoor area of the site known as the "*a-kalyptos,*" meaning "without cover." Over the years the *akalyptos* ended up as a rather unwholesome vacant space, surrounded by the bland party walls of neighboring buildings, signifying the unholy alliance of stifling planning regulations with maximum profit development.

Krokos, however, by eagerly investing an equal amount of care in the neglected atrium as to the building proper, had managed to create an enticing new raised court, entirely different than anything done before. By resurfacing the uneven surrounding walls, after agreement with the

neighbors, he framed and protected the internal outdoor area, and by the use of a skylight he allowed natural light to enter the gallery below, a rare gesture inside an asphyxiating city. The whole space is carved out and remodelled cautiously, using a variety of materials and

1. Johann Wolfgang von Goethe, *Satyros, Act 4* (1773), in *Goethean Science*, Rudolf Steiner, transl. William Lindeman, Mercury Press, 1988, pp.8-9.

2. Savas Condaratos and Wilfried Wang (eds.), *Architecture of the 29th c.: Greece*, Prestel, DAM, Hellenic Institute of Architecture, 1999, p.79-88.

3. See introduction to the Greek edition of Kenneth Frampton's *Modern Architecture: A Critical History of Modern Architecture.*

finishes (concrete, stone, mosaic, brick, plaster) from a color palette of earthy grays, reds and ochres. These, seemingly minor design choices are mentioned as an introduction to Krokos' characteristic design method, which involved, to the best of his abilities, the utilization of elements found on site, in order to improve the quality and character of the space.

Built by a civil engineer during the years 1979–1983, on a quid pro quo system, the typical five-storey building is located at the busy junction of Chiou and Metaxa streets in a central transitional area of Athens, near the main train station, surrounded by other similar apartment blocks and hotels. Krokos treated the prosaic existing apartment block literally as raw building matter, in order to transform it into an entirely new building entity with minimum structural intervention. The brief of the Fassianos Building was not, however for a typical apartment block, but called for a small museum-gallery that would house and exhibit the well-known painter Alekos Fassianos' paintings and prints, as well as apartments for his brothers, the musicians Andreas and Pavlos, and the actor Spyros. These apartments which occupy the second, third and fourth floors above Fassianos' apartment—though of the same area and aspect—follow slightly different spatial arrangements according to each brother's needs. Since its completion in 1995, the building was occasionally inhabited by the painter's brothers, but since the death of the pianist Andreas Fassianos, only Pavlos, who teaches guitar, lives there.

The gallery expands on four levels. The basement, which is naturally lit at the two ends by a skylight and by the semi-opaque staircase window, is one of the exhibition areas; it also contains a storage space for paintings and prints. The double-height ground floor is the main exhibition area, lit by the same skylight and by a series of clerestory windows at the perimeter. An internal mezzanine floor balcony on one side of the ground floor is also an exhibition area with additional wall storage for paintings. Lastly, the first floor above the gallery, which opens out on the aforementioned internal court and is accessed through both the small staircase from the mezzanine and from the main apartment ladder, will eventually be used as an exhibition area.

In addition to remodeling its interior spaces and the internal core, Krokos also redesigned the street facades by reframing the distinct horizontal balconies into two unified orthogonal frames. He also replaced the ground floor glazed surfaces by building a concrete wall, with a band of small clerestory windows above, in order to provide the necessary exhibition wall area inside. Thus the two functions of the new building are clearly expressed on its exterior. The solidity of the ground and mezzanine floors echoes their public gallery function, while the framed balconies above restate the apartment block typology as a joint expression of the brothers' residences. This duality of public (gallery) / private (apartments), reminiscent of Adolf Loos' treatment of his

Michaelerplatz Haus in Vienna is also carried through to the two entrances. Their symmetry is broken by slight adjustments and contrasts in their dimensions and materials, which denote their different functions: recessed versus protruding, framed versus uniform, solid versus transparent, flat versus raised. For example, the entrance to the museum and the entrance to the apartments, respectively, are different in all aspects. Their "split" is marked further by a round concrete column, which in place of a capital has a small gold recess that symbolizes the special character of the building.

The building is introverted, animated by the natural light coming through the atrium. Its interiors are served by a dual circulation system at the two corners of the building: a built main staircase and an elevator for the apartments, and an open metal staircase for the gallery spaces. Natural light plays an important role in the character of these staircases. In the apartment staircase, a secondary white skin curves over the existing wall surface, so as to let light through

Museum of Byzantine Culture, Thessaloniki
Kyriakos Krokos, 1978–93

variously shaped windows, a round one among them, like a sundial. The curved metal staircase in the galleries accepts light smoothly through a large sandblasted glass window that screens the interior from the street outside. Its window sill is formed into a series of concrete steps so as to carry the light downwards in a graded manner below into the basement gallery. The resulting archetypal, pyramidal form, like a miniature of the great staircase of Phaistos and reminiscent of Scarpa's detailing, brings the concrete to life, and reminds us of Louis Kahn's poetic description of matter as being "spent light."[4]

Such an approach to an existing structure is unique, at least within the contemporary Greek context, where most often neighboring buildings are either ignored as being worthless or slavishly imitated in the case of conservation. Krokos instead conceives of this project not as a self-enclosed building entity, determined solely by his clients' demands, but as a continuum of interior and exterior space and as part of the wider spatial environment. Although the Museum of Byzantine Culture in Thessaloniki is generally considered to be Krokos' masterpiece of his albeit short-lived career, the Fassianos Building is paradigmatic in convincingly demonstrating the architect's ability to transform successfully even a banal building into a disciplined and lyrical space within an urban context, and therein lays its value.[5]

The Art of Making: Slowness and Articulation

"There is a secret bond between slowness and memory, between speed and forgetting. Consider this utterly commonplace situation: a man is walking down the street. At a certain moment, he tries to recall something, but the recollection escapes him. Automatically, he slows down. Meanwhile, a person who wants to forget a disagreeable incident he has just lived through starts unconsciously to speed up his pace, as if he were trying to distance himself from a thing still too close to him in time."

— Milan Kundera[6]

4. "I sense Light as the giver of all presences, and material as spent light." from *Silence and Light I* (1968), published in *Louis Kahn Essential Texts*, Robert Twombly (ed.), WW Norton & Company, 2003, p. 229.

5. Kyriakos Krokos was born in 1941 and died in 1998. The Museum of Byzantine Culture was awarded a special prize in the first Greek Architectural Awards of 2000, being of unique value in contemporary Greek architecture, which though it has many first class residential buildings to be proud of (e.g. Nicos Valsamakis' own residence in Philothei which adorns the cover of the *100 Houses for 100 Architects*, P. Gössel (ed.), G. Postiglione, Taschen, 2004), it fairs rather poorly in the public sector.
6. Milan Kundera, *Slowness*, Harper Collins Publishers, 1996, p.39.

Modern Greek architecture already has its host of heroes to fall upon, from Dimitris Pikionis and Aris Konstantinidis to Nicos Valsamakis and Dimitris and Suzanna Antonakakis and many others. If Krokos belongs to this lineage of great architects, he is in a sense unique among them because of his painfully slow and caring approach to design, which is reflected in his buildings and that is so demanding so as to make it very hard to have a "school" of followers, in the current conditions of rapid production.[7] In fact, if one were to single out another unique post-war Greek architect, it would be Takis Zenetos, who, at the extreme opposite end of the spectrum, was a great innovator of advanced technology and transparency. Krokos would rarely refer to Zenetos, most likely because of the distance between them but also, I imagine, out of respect,[8] since, despite their obvious differences, they were both completely dedicated to an uncompromising architecture of the highest quality.

Such a comparison is useful, because it sets the context within which contemporary architects find themselves hard pressed to make choices between, on the one hand, by an ultra-modernist sensibility and on the other, by a sensitivity rooted on tradition. Although the issues they face have the same starting point—namely the burden on contemporary man that global changes at an unprecedented speed bring about—their reactions to them are critically different. One may observe a similar dichotomy in the answers given to the same problem in other arts. For example, whereas for Italo Calvino two primary concepts that will help us navigate through the future are Lightness and Quickness,[9] for Milan Kundera, in his highly charged erotic stories, it is Slowness that supports Memory against Speed, which brings about Forgetfulness.[10] Krokos chooses the second path, mentioning Matisse when he says, "One feels freer when one realizes that his efforts are recompensed by a tradition, be it as old as it may: this helps us take the jump over the ditch."[11]

Building for Krokos was a matter of conscience, as it was for Jože Plečnik, the great Slovenian architect of Ljubljana; this is what sets both of these very different architects apart from easy consumption. Leti Arvaniti-Krokou's description here of Krokos' long and demanding manner of working which she calls "a long labor," bears an uncanny similarity to a description of Plečnik, whose "incontestable originality" is perplexed by his relationship to contemporary life, which "is full of misunderstanding and sorrow." Furthermore,

Secondary School Agios Dimitrios, Athens
Takis Zenetos, 1970–76

"creatively, he is concerned with producing variations on the same idea, which he submits to a profound reflection for each occasion.... Due to the constraint of this self-critique, Plečnik can only create slowly and painfully; he attempts to clarify the logic of each detail, and it s only after having elaborated each and every element, in what might

7. See also Yorgos Tzirtzilakis "The Anthropological dimension in Kyriakos Krokos' buildings," *TA NEA* newspaper, 4 March 2000, p.6.
8. Krokos on Zenetos: "There is loneliness in our place. What you do is not set in a wider functioning context and that is why one is often in danger of being trodden on. Think of the demolition of Zenetos' FIX (brewery). The creation of architecture is a lonesome act." Mentioned in "Matter and Light," Kyriakos Krokos in conversation with Andreas Giacumacatos, *Design + Art in Greece*, No. 27 / 1996, pp.18-23.

9. Italo Calvino's *Six Memos for the Next Millennium* (Charles Eliot Norton Lectures 1985-86, Vintage, 1993) are the following: Lightness, Quickness, Exactitude, Visibility, Multiplicity and Consistency.
10. See Milan Kundera's *The Unbearable Lightness of Being* (1984) and especially *Slowness* (op. cit.), where memory is also described as the only antidote to the excesses of power and authoritarianism.
11. Krokos in *A. Fassianos – K. Krokos, Architectonika Topia*, Nireas, 1987, p. 6 (author's translation).

appear to be an excessively meticulous fashion, that he moves towards the completion of a work.... The decisive factor is not for him the form as such, but its logic and intention."[12]

This is why his projects "have for all intents and purposes, no influence on the development of architecture and on public opinion. The eminent talent remains without an echo...."[13]

One could also mention the elective affinities of Krokos to such great "proto-modernist" architects as Otto Wagner, Peter Behrens, Auguste Perret, and Hendrik Petrus Berlage. Indeed his proximity to some of them, as well as to Adolf Loos, Louis Kahn, Luis Barragán, and Tadao Ando has already been rightly noted by the historian Andreas Giacumacatos and by Krokos himself.[14] What brings such diverse personalities together are not the formal qualities of their work but their common conviction that architecture as a design process is inseparable from the art of building. Hence, the discipline of architecture is a manner of art that is continuously informed by making and incorporating contemporary technology without ever abandoning high quality craftsmanship.

Krokos' regression[15] from what could be described as the "speed" of modern culture ("speed" of information, "speed" of effect, "speed" of form[16]), which is the mark of our times since Marinetti's praise of velocity, seems to be going against the grain. But this is an intentional restraint of an architect who is interested more in the "secret bond between slowness and memory" rather than "to speed and forgetfulness." By deliberately staying outside the current state of "liquid modernity,"[17] Krokos gains a critical distance from contemporary preoccupations and directs himself towards the discerning study of architecture in the *specific circumstances* of its making in a *particular place*.

This desire sets him apart even from Dimitris Pikionis, the architect he admires most. Krokos' almost compulsive control on form through geometry and detailing seems to be his answer in finding the proper limits to design. By exhaustively planning everything he adheres to a classicizing approach, leaving nothing to chance. In this way he wishes to overcome the limits of place or style, allowing only for time to affect space and matter beyond the architect's control. Though references to Pikionis both by Krokos and his critics justly abound, his work is also distinct from Pikionis in important ways. Despite Krokos' weaving a thread like Ariadne's to get out of the labyrinth of modernism, he uses current building techniques, such as concrete frame construction which he tries to express clearly by boldly making an asset of it. Krokos acknowledges Pikionis as being a paragon for contemporary Greek architecture when he says, "Today it would be wrong for someone to return to the folk culture, today there is Pikionis.... today there is no more folk culture."[18] But at the same time, Krokos recognizes that the circumstances—social, urban and technical—after the 1960s and 70s, are no longer the same.

Prague castle additions, Hradčany Prague
Jože Plečnik, 1927–31

12. Mentioned by Vladimir Šlapeta in *Jože Plečnik, Architect 1872–1957*, François Burkhardt, Claude Eveno and Boris Podrecca (eds.), transl. Carol Volk, The MIT Press, 1989, p. 85.
13. *Ibid*,
14. Andreas Giacumacatos, Curator of Krokos' participation at the VI International Exhibition of Architecture (1996 Venice Biennale) and author of a monograph on Krokos (*Design + Art in Greece*, No. 27 / 1996), has also published in the same volume an illuminating conversation with Krokos, which verifies and reinforces through his own words many of these points ("Matter and Ligh," op.cit.).
15. "So I gave up magazines, around the mid-70s, when I took part in the competition for the museum. I did not want to start by what is or is not architecture, what are these -isms that you are referring to, to be part of them.... Nowadays I look in my own way at some magazines. I am not interested in belonging somewhere." From "Matter and Light," op. cit. (author's translation).
16. On the opposite end of the quest for speed, witness the current "slow" movements, such as the "slow food" movement against "fast food," "slow" money, "slow" art, even "slow" architecture.
17. Zygmunt Bauman, *Liquid Modernity*, Polity Press 2000.
18. "Matter and Light," op. cit. (author's translation).

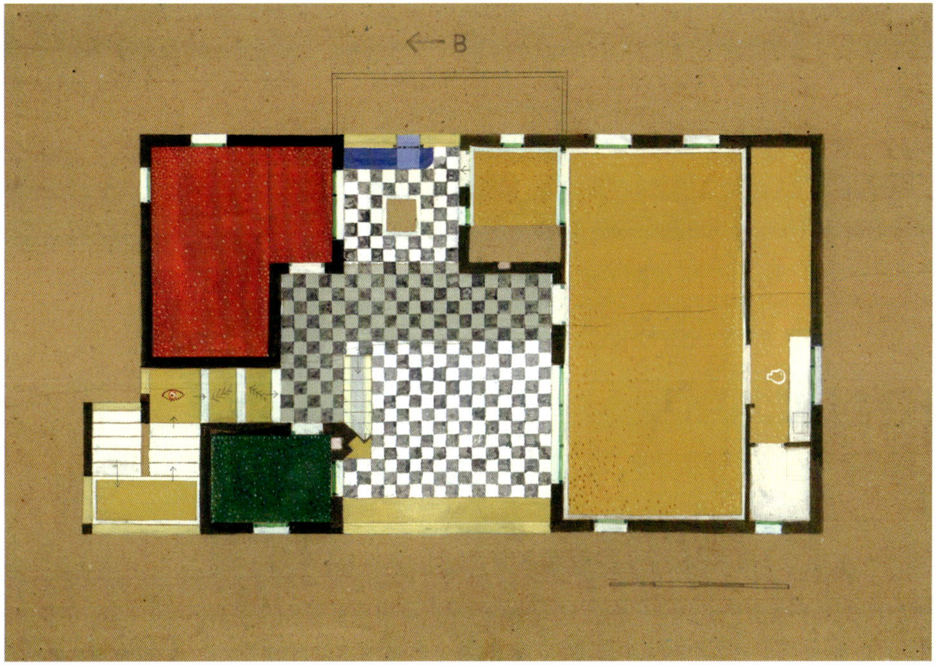

Sketches for Fassianos Atelier, Papagou, Athens
Kyriakos Krokos, 1995

In this way, although both of their rejection of modernism is common in their critique of its rigid functionalism and indifference to place, Krokos' search for all that is genuine in the vernacular runs a very different course from that of Pikionis. Pikionis turns to fragments of the folk vernacular that he weaves into his designs, using the rural house of Rodakis[19] in Aegina as a paradigm. Krokos on the other hand, looks in the direction of the popular urban neoclassicism of craftsmen builders (e.g., in the 19th century school in Samos), because of its discipline, order, and sense of decorum. He even admits that the modern 1930s buildings in Athens are some of the best, for they have the same material qualities of articulation.[20] The everyday vernacular is present in both of these architects, but the way in which it is absorbed and its elements are incorporated into their work is very different.

For Pikionis the search leads to a picturesque manner of composition, which reaches its zenith in the landscaping of the approach to the Acropolis and Philopappou and its nadir in the Potamianos residence in Philothei; his spirit is always that of a collector, a bricoleur of memories. Krokos,

19. Pikionis first stressed the virtues of the house built in Aegina island by the farmer Alecos Rodakis, at the end of the 18th century. See Klaus Vrieslander, Giulio Caimi, *To spiti tou Rodaki stin Aegina* (The Rodakis house in Aegina), Akritas, 1997 (in Greek).

20. "Matter and Light," *ibid.*

Paving stones on approach to the Acropolis, Athens
Dimitris Pikionis, 1954–57, from Archives Dimitris Pikionis

however, remains firmly a designer, a constructor, and a builder who organizes geometrically all parts within a composition so that they are rationally bonded together. He reminds us of the Loosian definition of the architect as the educated master builder who could speak Latin, or in this case, Greek.

Just as he conceives design as being part of the building process, so form is content. Its articulation is a way to

Window latch detail, Fassianos Building, Athens
Kyriakos Krokos, 1995

show the content through the form. His attention to detailing is extraordinary, though it is not fetishistic. Aris Konstantinidis whom Krokos also esteemed, scared him because he is too dogmatic, while Krokos, despite his perfectionism, admits that he loves open-ended things, not closed, that he "loves mistakes."[21]

When visiting the Fassianos Building along with Wilfried Wang and Thomas Herzog for the first time, I was surprised at Herzog's admiration of the detailing, especially as his work displays an equal amount of attention to construction. Herzog, on noticing my surprise, explained that that the reason he admired Krokos' details in the Fassianos house (some of which were made with the collaboration of Alekos Fassianos) were not standardized like his own. Instead, they were conceived as the appropriate and often unique answers to specific problems, even the minutest having an important role to play within the whole. "Ornament is the adoration of the joint,"[22] Louis Kahn stated unequivocally, an aphorism Krokos would readily subscribe to. Significantly, the discussion arose around the observation of a simple but elegant tiny metal triangular latch for the windows.

"Materials must speak," Krokos also contends, but he points out that the key to our success lies in the way they are related to one another.[23] Krokos' preference for a slow and thoughtful procedure is an attempt to actually look at things, rather than simply glance at them running past us at shutter speed. Even the way we speak about what we do matters. Constructing and building do not mean the same thing.

"It seems to me that little by little we have forgotten to construct … Building means

21. "Matter and Light," *ibid.*

22. Louis Kahn, *Light is the Theme*, Kimbell Art Museum Publication Two, 1975, p.43.

23. "Materials must speak. This I consider obvious. Otherwise the building, whatever its arrangements, remains lifeless. Matter must express itself." "Matter and Light," *ibid.*

assembling homogeneous elements, constructing means tying together hetero-geneous elements. 'Cezanne constructed, did not build—building means stuffing.' That is how Braque speaks. Let us think about that."[24]

Krokos' expressive use of solid masonry materials also aims to make buildings that look decent at every stage of their construction. Krokos wanted to avoid what he often described as a series of burials during which, each building task covers the traces of the next—the painter burying the plasterer's work, the plasterer the electrician's and the plumber's and so on—and he wished for his buildings to be as clean as a pebble after the water washed it off. Krokos worked to respect the practice of building at all times and show it for what it is. The rooftop drainage in the Fassianos Building illustrates his approach beautifully. When he has to deal with such a commonplace problem as getting rid of the water from a rooftop, Krokos designed a gently slanting canal that starts at its apex, at the corner of the building, and gradually falls down along the perimeter, lowering on both sides, effortlessly disposing of the rainwater. The mundane function is transformed into a rational and aesthetically pleasing solution to the problem.

While many Greek architects admire the beauty in our unfinished skeletal constructions (the "*yapi*" as it is called, using a Turkish word for the concrete frame of the building), Krokos was really one of the first Greek architects to explicitly recognize its aesthetic value and put it to use in his buildings. "Basic materials [are] concrete and brick—it is an image I have before apartment buildings are plastered, when they show their minor truth.... I accepted their challenge."[25]

Such widespread building methods that have been the norm in Greece over the last century (concrete frame with brick infill) are rarely exposed. They are generally considered to be too humble and so they are expediently hidden behind plaster and paint. In the Fassianos Building though, as well as in many of Krokos' other residences along with his small Cykladon Street Theatre, Krokos uses exposed brickwork, following even the practice of inclined bricks on the upper string course, so that it becomes "ornament." By leaving such building elements unadorned he elevates materials into a type of metaphysics of building. Again, as expressed by Louis Kahn:

"To express is to drive. And when you want to give something presence, you have to consult nature. And there is where Design comes in. And if you think of Brick, for instance, and you say to Brick, 'What do you want Brick?'

Vettas Residence, Philothei, Athens
Kyriakos Krokos, 1989–91

And Brick says to you, 'I like an Arch.' And if you say to Brick, 'Look, arches are expensive, and I can use a concrete lintel over you. What do you think of that?' 'Brick?' Brick says: '... I like an Arch.'"[26]

24. *Tefchos* No. 2 / 1989, p.47 (author's translation).

25. Krokos' thoughts on the design of the Byzantine Museum, *Tefchos*, op. cit., p.48 (author's translation).

26. Louis Kahn in John Lobell, *Between Silence and Light: Spirit in the Architecture of Louis I. Kahn*, Shambala Publications, 1979, p. 40. On the etymology and importance of ornament (*diakosmos*) in architecture see also: Panayotis A. Michelis, *Architecture as an Art*, Panayotis & Effie Michelis Foundation, 2002.

Indian Institute of Management, Ahmedabad
Louis I. Kahn, 1962–74

Muuratsalo Summer House, Muuratsalo,
Alvar Aalto, 1952

Krokos' architecture is in fact a manifestation of his care for the tactile as well as visual aspects of space, as his fascination with the finishes of his building surfaces reveals. The walls of the Fassianos Building are a veritable sampling of concrete, brick, and plaster finishes, in relief or in recess, an almost hedonistic attempt to endow each space with the appropriate ambience that different materials can offer, as light strikes their surface. His sensibility is reminiscent of Alvar Aalto's Muuratsalo Lake House of 1952, where he used a variety of different techniques for brickwork. Like Berlage or Perret before them, Aalto and Krokos were trying to find the correct way to build with brick or to make concrete—a useful but formless material—into a proper tectonic component. As concrete can be poured into any shape, Krokos takes advantage of this process and even plays with the possibilities: along with Fassianos he placed a watermelon within the concrete bench in the courtyard, that when taken out (and eaten!) formed the built-in sink bowl. This literal immersion of his design process in the act of building explains why he so often spoke, in his occasional lectures or interviews, of the relationship on-site with his builders, especially with the one who framed, poured and treated the concrete.

Krokos found it essential to develop his thinking about architecture through the building activity and let his architectural language speak through that development, ennobling even an "a-tectonic" material like the much scorned and debased concrete. In his workers' hands, concrete is refined in so many ways—shiny, rough, smooth or textured—so that the finished surface resembles the treatment of stone and of fine plastered surfaces. For Krokos, building is a moral matter. "I am thinking of the ethos that is required by the correct articulation of a wall, the rhythm it imposes."[27]

Solidity and Serenity

"Any work of architecture which does not express serenity is a mistake. That is why it has been an error to replace the protection of walls with today's intemperate use of enormous glass windows."[28]

—Luis Barragán

The pregnant silence of building that Barragán attributes to solidity in his gently aphoristic criticism of modernism, and which he shared with his friend Louis Kahn, is a quality that Krokos, an admirer of both these architects, also seeks in his architecture. The solidity of building that offers security to its inhabitants, brings memories of old, time-honored structures and leads to peacefulness. Serenity—as an important quality of architecture that endures and is also found in the work of other Greek architects such as Nicos Valsamakis—is frequently juxtaposed by Dimitris Fatouros against the formally excessive current trend for frantic and aggressive new forms.[29]

In the Fassianos Building Krokos choose not to impose an extravagant form on the existing structure but to re-think its material and spatial logic in order to discover the most appropriate forms and proportions for it. His desire to create buildings that are neither eye-catching nor provocatively flaunting themselves at us, results in an architecture that, while seemingly austere, is also highly lyrical and almost indifferent to contemporary discourse. The serenity achieved by solidity is also enlivened by the play of light and shadow, thus becoming "light" in the sense of being weightless, because its surfaces are an offering to light. This tranquility that is missing from our fast-tracking century is to be found in the walls built by architects not just in order to restrict and separate, but in order to protect and bring together in space, in the most considered manner, the anguished and alienated contemporary man. In these walls also resides perhaps an element of melancholy, an evasive state of being, which is not usually associated with practical, architectural endeavors, but is visible in the metaphysical cityscapes of De Chirico, as well as in the landscape paintings of Krokos. Krokos' sense of color, his earthy, melancholy shades, he owes to his teacher and mentor in Paris, the Greek painter Yannis Tsarouchis. Color in his buildings is created by matter itself, from within the constructional process, not as an add-on, but as a necessary corollary to the building. It is interesting that when Krokos speaks of texture and light, he refers more frequently to painters than to architects as sources of inspiration, from Georges Braque, Henri Matisse, Paul Cezanne and Jan Vermeer to the Greek Yannis Moralis.

It was late one spring afternoon as the sun was setting down in 1996, when the concept of melancholy as a prerequisite to great architecture according to Plečnik,[30] unexpectedly came to my mind. I mentioned it to Krokos, asking for his opinion. I had just met him for the first time in his house-atelier under the Acropolis in order to invite him for a lecture at the school where I was then teaching, and we had spent a few hours talking and getting to know each other.[31] As the day drew to its close Krokos replied, "This I will have to think about," and fell into a prolonged, thoughtful silence. This reflection upon a sentence, upon a thought, or upon a pebble, is,

27. Kyriakos Krokos, in *Architecture in Greece* No. 23 /1989, p. 120 (author's translation).
28. Emilio Ambasz, *The Architecture of Luis Barragán*, The Museum of Modern Art, New York, 1976, p.8.

29. See Dimitris Fatouros' recent books: *I Epimoni tis Architektonikis* (The Persistence of Architecture) Kastaniotis, 2007 and *Ichni Metavasis* (Traces of Transition), Kastaniotis, 2009.

30. Jan Kotěra, the great Czech architect, a friend of Plečnik and also a student of Otto Wagner, characterized Plečnik's work as being touched with "simplicity and melancholy." Plečnik himself, while commenting enthusiastically on a text by Kotěra had noted on his part, that, "only it is unfortunately that for my tastes—and I have so much confidence in you—at times you lack a touch of melancholy.' Jože Plečnik, *ibid.*, p. 84.
31. AKTO Art & Design College, Athens, Greece.

I think, characteristic of the man. Krokos would not hasten but rather wait in order to answer rigorously when the time was right, as he did with his designs and buildings. In Krokos' case, as in all great artists, it seems to be difficult to separate the work from the man, as George Makris, his long time friend and collaborator has insightfully noted.[32]

The joy and melancholy of nature comes forcefully through Krokos' buildings and paintings, as the setting of life, rather than as their imitation. One of the most famous photographs of his buildings is the rooftop of a house in Aegina, which appears as a series of "ground" platforms set in a cloudy landscape by the sea. Krokos believed that "nature without any human signs always induced awe," and he was only attracted by a landscape when he could intimate the presence of a human artifact within it.[33] One senses this in looking at his work from above, where from a vantage point of a roof terrace—be it the first Fassianos atelier in Cholargos or the Vettas residence in Philothei—one can see the careful and exact planning of raised and recessed steps, paving tiles, and marble slabs, that gives order to the dense weaving of trees, plants, and flower gardens and to every possible path or place of contemplation within them.

32. See George Makris, "Gia ton Kyriako Kroko," in the *Memorial* volume on Krokos' drawings and paintings, published posthumously by his wife Leti Arvaniti-Krokou (Ikaros, 2008, pp.9-12, in Greek).
33. *Architectonika Topia, ibid.*, p. 5 (author's translation).

So in the end one wonders, through this journey in one man's work, if there is, after all, a disparity between a sense of being contemporaneous and a sense of being timeless. As Fassianos himself points out here in this book, the fact is that Krokos' buildings age well, letting time to take its toll in due course. The walls of brick and concrete that wear slowly, or the balconies of bronze that oxidize quickly, are all manifestations that bear the mark of time. As Kyriakos Krokos's poignantly said, "The ruins of a hut and the ruins of a temple are harmonized to the same extent within nature. The building which is perishable and at the same time eternal, returns its materials to the earth that gave birth to them, in contrast to contemporary buildings that grow old ugly."[34] This attribute of ageing gently and gracefully is also to be found in romantic conceptions of architecture, such as in Bertolt Brecht's poem "Of all the Works of Man";

"...Half ruined buildings once again take on
The look of buildings waiting to be finished
Generously planned: their fine proportions
Can already be guessed at, but they still
Need our understanding. At the same time
They have already served, indeed have already
been overcome.
All this
Delights me."[35]

34. *Architectonika Topia, ibid.*, p. 7 (my translation).
35. Bertolt Brecht, *Vin allen Werken*, 1932. (English transl., *Of all the Works of Man*, in Reinhold Grimm (ed.) Caroline Molina y Vedia (coll), Bertolt Brecht: *Poetry and Prose*, The Continuum International Publishing Group Inc, 2003).

It may sound strange here, but the aim of all the Moderns, from the Constructivists to the Neoplasticists, was to bring art and life indelibly together. So, in the case of Krokos, and in this most exemplary edifice for Alekos Fassianos, the pleasure and melancholy of building is reflected in the pleasure and melancholy of living. In George Seferis words, the poet laureate fro whom Krokos had a high regard, houses always had that particular quality of endurance, even obstinacy:

"I don't know much about houses,
I remember their joy and their sorrow
sometimes, when I stop to think;
Houses, you know, grow resentful easily when
you strip them bare."[36]

36. George Seferis, "Thrush (I. The house near the sea)" (1946), in *George Seferis: Collected Poems*, translated, edited and introduced by Edmund Keeley and Philip Sherrard, Princeton University Press, 1995.

Vettas Residence, Athens
Kyriakos Krokos, 1989–91

Photographs

ΓΕΝΙΚΗ
ΕΞΟΠΛΙΣΜΟΣ

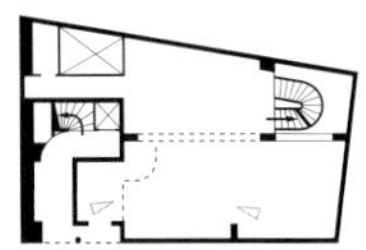

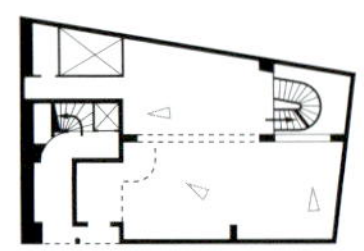

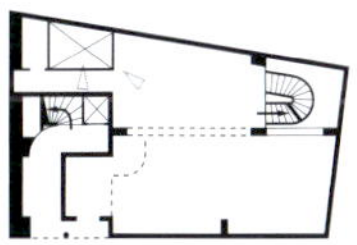

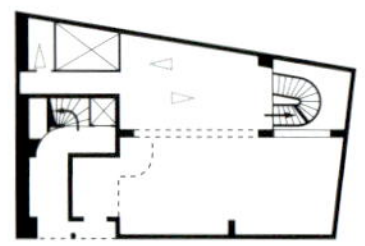

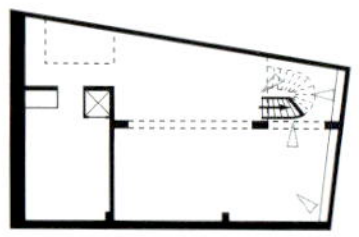

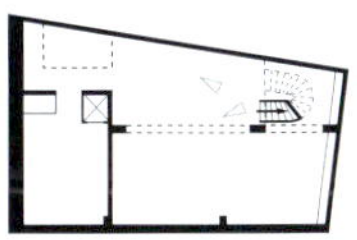

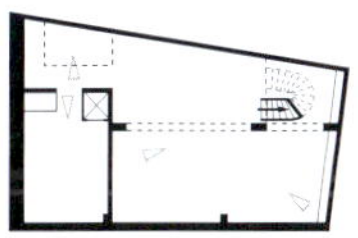

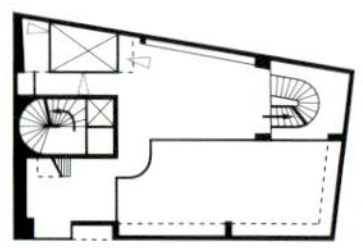

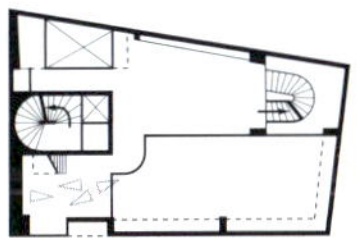

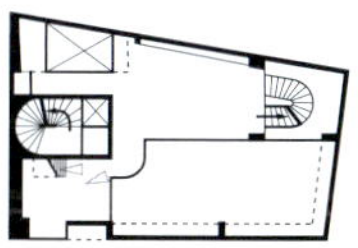

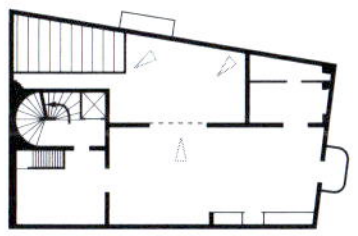

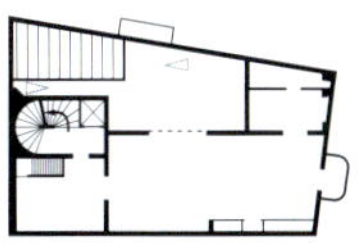

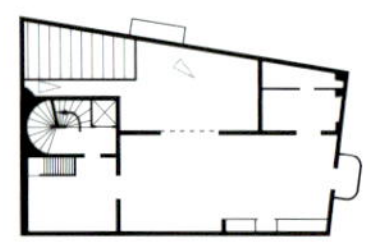

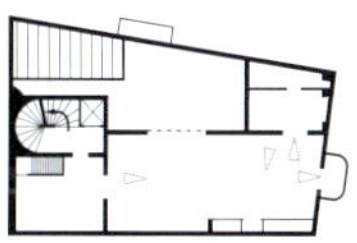

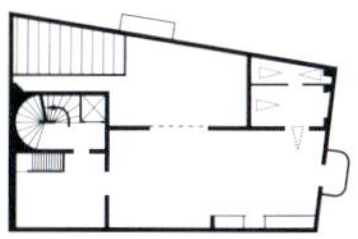

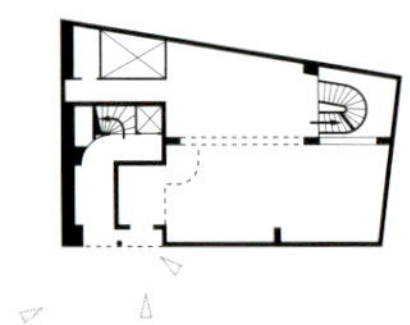

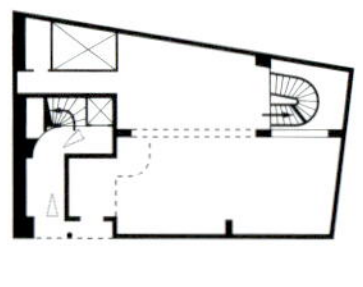

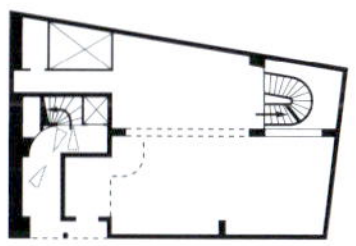

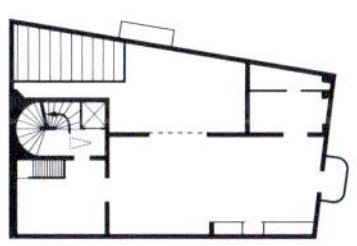

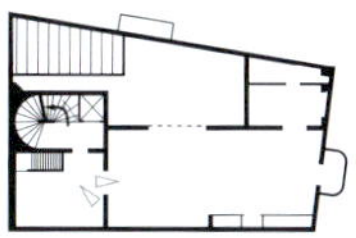

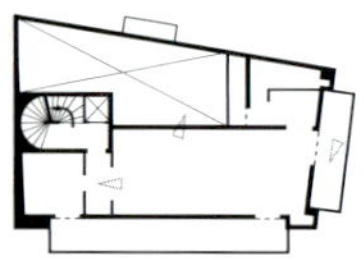

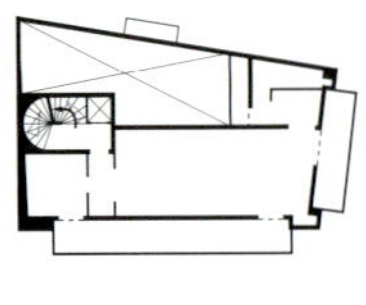

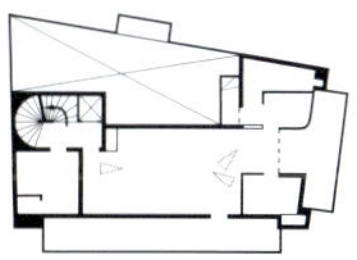

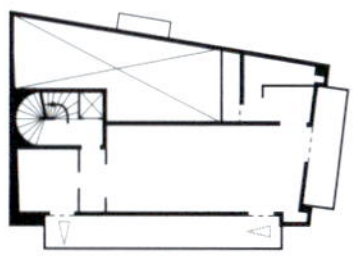

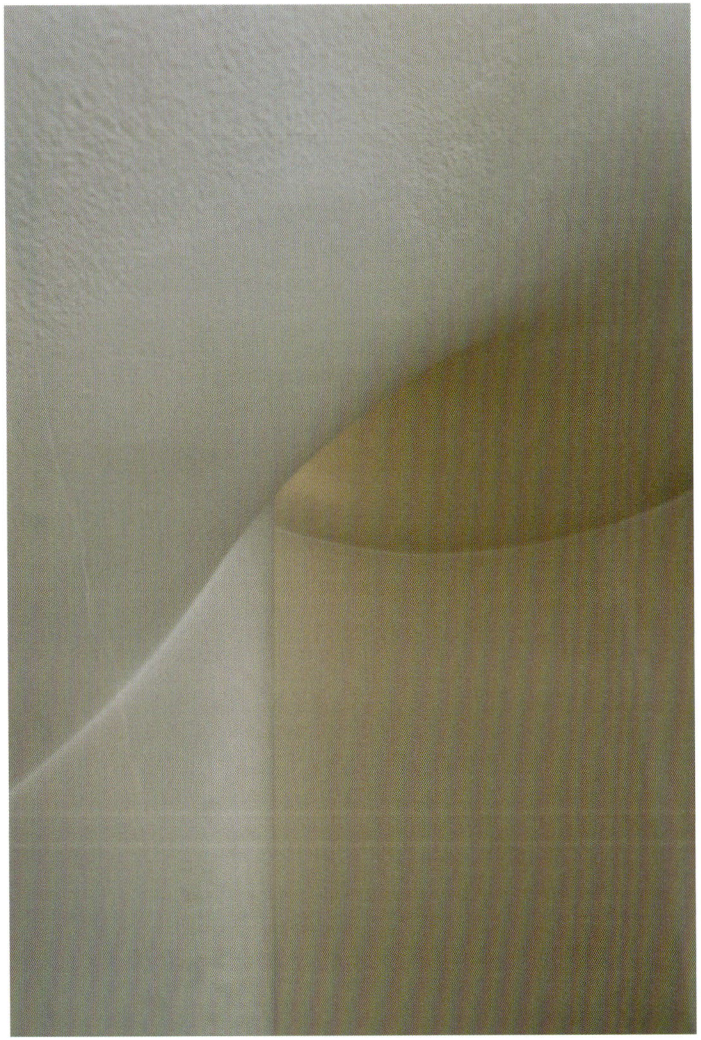

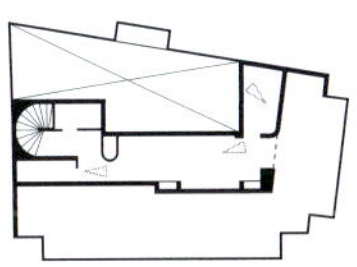

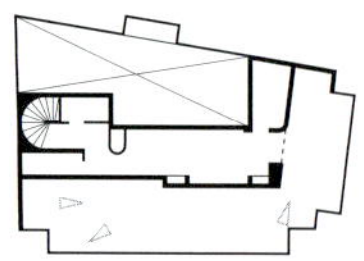

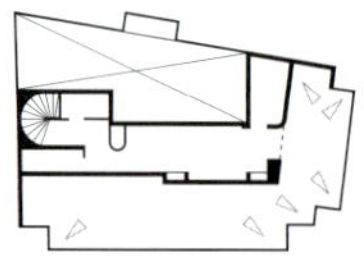

Biographies

Leti Arvaniti-Krokou

Leti Arvaniti-Krokou, born in Athens, studied architecture at the National Technical University of Athens, graduating in 1983. She met Kyriakos Krokos during her studies and from 1984 onwards worked with him at his office, being closely involved in the important projects.

Leti Arvaniti and Kyriakos Krokos married in 1985 and had three children. After Krokos' untimely death in 1998, she decided to close the office, transforming it into the house where she is now living with their children.

Since 2001 she has been working at the Neohellenic Architectural Archives of the Benaki Museum in Athens, which holds a large collection of 19th and 20th century Greek architects' archives.

In 2008, ten years after of Krokos' death, Arvaniti-Krokou organized an exhibition showing some of his sketches and drawings at the Astra gallery in Athens. She was the editor of the catalogue that included these drawings and four texts written by close acquaintances of Krokos; the catalogue is entitled *For Kyriakos Krokos — Remembrance.*

Elias Constantopoulos

Elias Constantopoulos studied at the Bartlett School of Architecture, University College London (1975–81). He has been in private practice in Athens since 1986 and was director of Sigma Design Ltd (1990–95), receiving a State Prize for Industrial Design.

He has been teaching in Athens since 1989 and is currently Associate Professor in Architecture and Interior Design at the Department of Architecture, University of Patras. He is a member of *Do.Co.Mo.Mo.* and board member of the Hellenic Institute of Architects as well as the Hellenic Society of Aesthetics.

Elias Constantopoulos was co-editor of *9H* (London) and *Ntizain* (Athens) magazines and is consultant editor of the reviews *Architecture in Greece* and *Design + Art in Greece*. He has published numerous articles and monographs on contemporary architecture, art and design, as well as the books *Nikos Valsamakis, Architect 1950-1983; Contemporary Industrial Design in Greece: History of Applied Arts; Aegean: A Dispersed Urbanity;* and *ON: The Modern and the Contemporary in European and Japanese Culture*. He was also the consultant editor of *Architecture of the 20th Century: Greece.*

Alekos Fassianos

Alekos Fassianos, born in 1935, is a renowned Greek painter. Fassianos draws his subjects from Greek mythology, Byzantine icons and the shadow theater.

Fassianos studied violin at the Athens Conservatoire, painting at the Athens School of Fine Arts (1956–1960), where he was taught by Yannis Moralis, and lithography in Paris (1960–1963), on a French state scholarship. From 1960 to 2002 he divided his time between Paris and Athens. Since his first Athens exhibition in 1959 he has had more than 70 personal exhibitions in cities including Paris, Athens, Thessaloniki, Milan, New York, London, Tokyo, Beirut, Hamburg, and Munich.

Apart from painting, he has been involved in book illustration, poster design (including posters and stamps for the Athens Olympics in 2004), and theatre design. He has also written collections of poems and essays. His works are exhibited in museums and private collections in Greece and abroad and have been presented in Greek and French television documentaries.

Wilfried Wang

Wilfried Wang is the O'Neil Ford Centennial Professor in Architecture at The University of Texas at Austin. Together with Barbara Hoidn, he is founder of the office of Hoidn Wang Partner, Berlin.

Wang studied architecture in London, where he was in partnership with John Southall. In 1979 he was founding co-editor of the *9H* magazine and co-director of the 9H Gallery from 1985 to 1990. From 1995 to 2000 he was director of the German Architecture Museum.

He taught at the Polytechnic of North London, University College London, ETH Zurich, Harvard University and University of Navarra.

Wang is the author of various architectural publications and has served on numerous competition and award juries. He is an honorary member of the Federation of German Architects, and a member of the Royal Swedish Academy of Arts, as well as the Academy of the Arts, Berlin.

Alekos Fassianos, sketch, pencil

Project Credits and Chronology

Project Credits

Architect	Kyriakos Krokos
Collaborators	Yota Kalavritinou
	Melina Chadjiyiannouli
Structural Engineer	Yannis Tsopanakis
Lighting Designer	Giorgos Fatseas
Artist	Alekos Fassianos
Stone mason	Fotis Vatelis
Carpenter	Dionisis Pettas
Metal worker	Dimitris Chatziorfanos
Pluming	Nikos Karagiorgos
Builders	Panagiotis Tsiakoumis
	Giorgos Panou
	Leonidas Diveris
	Takis Glykiotis
Client	Eleni Fassianou

Chronology

1989	Commission
May 1990	Application for Planning Permission
Autumn 1990	Commencement of Construction
1995	Completion of Construction

Kyriakos Krokos, Small House, crayon

Selected Bibliography

Condaratos, S., and Wang, W., eds. *20th-Century Architecture – Greece*, Hellenic Institute of Architecture/Deutsches-Architektur Museum. Munich: Prestel,1999.

Giacumacatos, A., ed. "Monographs VIII. Kyriakos Krokos." *Design + Art in Greece*, No. 27 (1996).

Giacumacatos, A., ed. *The Architect Kyriakos Krokos, Greek Exhibit at the VI International Architecture Exhibition, Venice Biennale*, Sep 15 – Nov 17, 1996. Venice.

Photo Credits

Cover: Wilfried Wang

Elias Constantopoulos: pages 10, 11, 12, 57 (left), 59, 62 (right), 63, 67, 80 (left), 81, 87 (left), 90, 92 (right), 94 (left), 95 (left), 97 (top, bottom left), 98 (left), 99, 101 (right), 106, 108 (left), 113 (right), 114 (left), 116 (right), 118 (bottom left), 119, 120 (right), 121 (left), 123, 125 (right), 128 (left), 129, 130, 136 (left).

Rory Hyde: page 60.

Charalambos Louizidis: pages 13, 17, 56, 58, 70 (left), 71 (right), 72, 93 (left), 100, 102 (top left), 110 (left), 124 (left), 128 (right), 137 (left), 138.

Dave Morris: page 64.

Daniel Sylvester: pages 16, 57 (right), 73 (right), 75, 76 (bottom left, right), 77, 79 (right), 80 (center, right), 82 (left), 84, 85, 86 (right), 87 (right), 88 (right), 89 (left), 91 (right), 93 (right), 95 (center, right), 96, 97 (right), 98 (right), 101 (left), 102 (top right), 103, 104, 105, 107 (center, right), 109 (right), 110 (right), 113 (left), 115, 117, 118 (top left), 120 (left), 122 (left), 125 (left, center), 127, 131 (left), 132, 133, 134, 135, 137 (left), 139.

Yorgos Tourkovassilis: 12, 70 (left top and bottom), 71 (left top and bottom), 74, 76 (top left), 78 (right), 79 (left), 92 (bottom), 94 (right), 102 (bottom), 112 (right).

Yorgos Vrettakos: pages 55, 73 (left), 114 (right), 121 (right), 122 (right), 136 (right).

Wilfried Wang: pages 78 (left), 82 (right), 83, 86 (left), 88 (left), 89 (right), 91 (left), 92 (left, center), 107 (left), 108 (right), 109 (left), 111, 112 (left), 116 (left), 118 (right), 124 (right), 126, 131 (right).

O'NFM 3